CHRISTIAN BELIEVING

CHRISTIAN BELIEVING

THE NATURE OF THE CHRISTIAN FAITH
AND ITS EXPRESSION
IN HOLY SCRIPTURE AND CREEDS

A Report by
The Doctrine Commission of
the Church of England

LONDON
SPCK

First published in 1976
by SPCK
Holy Trinity Church
Marylebone Road
London NW1 4DU

Printed in Great Britain by
The Camelot Press Ltd, Southampton
ISBN 0 281 02937 7

Contents

Acknowledgements

Thanks are due to the following for permission to quote from copyright sources:

James Clarke & Co. Ltd: *The Mystical Theology of the Eastern Church*, by Vladimir Lossky.

Editions Aubier Montaigne: *In the Image and Likeness of God*, by Vladimir Lossky.

SCM Press Ltd: *The Bible in the Modern World*, by James Barr.

Foreword by
The Archbishop of Canterbury

I take this opportunity of recording my thanks to the Chairman and members of the Doctrine Commission of the Church of England for the care with which they have examined *The Nature of the Christian Faith and its Expression in Holy Scripture and Creeds*. The unanimity of the report was not easily achieved, and the individual essays which comprise the latter part of the book show the variety of gifts and outlooks of the various contributors. That is indeed a source of enrichment for us who can now read the finished work.

Each generation needs men who, in honesty and devotion, are prepared to undertake 'exploration into God', to press beyond the confines of what hitherto we have grasped, and to move away from places that have become too narrow for us in the light of modern knowledge and experience. The members of the Commission have sought to do just this, and I for one am grateful.

DONALD CANTUAR:

Members of the Commission

The Reverend Dr M. F. Wiles: *Chairman*
Canon of Christ Church and Regius Professor of Divinity in the University of Oxford

The Reverend A. M. Allchin
Canon of Canterbury

The Reverend J. A. Baker
Canon of Westminster

The Reverend Dr J. G. Davies
Edward Cadbury Professor of Theology in the University of Birmingham

The Reverend C. F. Evans
Professor of New Testament Studies, University of London King's College

The Reverend E. M. B. Green
Rector of St Aldate's, Oxford

The Reverend J. L. Houlden
Principal of Ripon College, Cuddesdon

The Reverend C. P. M. Jones
Principal of Pusey House, Oxford

The Reverend D. R. Jones
Canon of Durham and Lightfoot Professor of Divinity in the University of Durham

The Reverend Dr G. W. H. Lampe
Regius Professor of Divinity in the University of Cambridge

J. R. Lucas
Tutor in Philosophy, Merton College, Oxford

The Reverend Dr J. I. Macquarrie
Canon of Christ Church and Lady Margaret Professor of Divinity in the University of Oxford

The Right Reverend Hugh Montefiore
Bishop of Kingston-upon-Thames

Preface

This has not been an easy report to write. The task that was given us was to say something about 'The Nature of the Christian Faith and its Expression in Holy Scripture and Creeds'. These are issues with which Christians have grappled down the ages and they pose particular problems today. Moreover the Commission itself includes a broad spectrum of the varied attitudes to these fundamental issues that are to be found within the Church of England.

We began our work under the chairmanship of Bishop Ian Ramsey. His death deprived us collectively of a wise chairman and severally of a much loved friend. We hope that he would not have been displeased with the final outcome of this work which he began.

The first half of our publication comprises a joint report carefully worked out and subscribed to by all the members of the Commission. It shows certain underlying agreements between us about the way in which Christians need to approach the question of belief, and especially the relation of belief today to its formulations in the past in the Bible and in the creeds. But the report also acknowledges the very considerable degree of divergence that exists within the Commission.

Two appendixes of a slightly more technical kind have been added to the report. One deals with the degree of unity and variety to be found within the New Testament itself, the other with the way in which the creeds originated and took their place in the life and worship of the Church.

Joint reports of this kind often make dull reading. So far as we have avoided this danger, the credit is wholly due to Canon Baker, who has drafted, and redrafted, our findings with a patience and skill that has won him the gratitude and admiration of his colleagues.

Even so, any report that draws together the views of so many varied individuals is bound to lack some of the liveliness and vigour that would characterize a single individual's expression of his own faith. In addition, therefore, to the general report we include individual essays on this same central issue by eight members of the Commission. These essays illustrate the variety of approach which we point to in the report and also serve to put flesh and blood on to the bare bones of the report itself.

Each essayist has written entirely for himself and the Commission as a whole is not committed to what any individual essayist has said. Moreover, the essays do not all set out to deal with the central issue in just the same way. Mr Lucas and Dr Nineham are concerned with the way in which questions of doctrine need to be approached today. They spell out more fully than was possible in the report itself two different approaches within the Church to the role to be played by the great formulations of the past in our understanding of faith today. In order to concentrate on questions of the method by which we need to work, they have very largely left on one side questions of the content of faith itself. The four essays that follow—by Canon Jones, Professor Lampe, Dr Turner, and myself—do not deal so directly with the question of method but seek rather to illustrate it by consideration of the central content of Christian belief. In the last two essays the primary emphasis is on the fact that Christian belief is something experienced, something lived. In Canon Allchin's essay the main stress is on the corporate experience of the whole Church, while Bishop Hugh Montefiore writes rather from the standpoint of a personal profession of faith.

We have written as a group of Anglicans for members of the Church of England. But the problems we discuss are common to all Christians. We hope that both what we have said jointly and the individual essays will prove of help to many Christians in their attempt to understand their faith better and to live it more faithfully.

MAURICE WILES
Chairman

JOINT REPORT

1

The Adventure of Faith

Christian life is an adventure, a voyage of discovery, a journey, sustained by faith and hope, towards a final and complete communion with the Love at the heart of all things. There are times in this life when the Christian finds in himself an ever deepening confidence which, even if it does not draw the sting of pain, difficulty, or sorrow, yet enables him to pass victoriously through them. This confidence brings with it an inner conviction, so strong that it can feel very like actual knowledge, about the reality of his goal and the rightness of his way. Life is not a puzzle of trying to find out whether the goal exists, and how to get to it if it does; it is an experience of being drawn by a love which most certainly does exist, and which by the power of its influence at any given moment confirms the right way towards itself. But equally, at the other extreme, there are times when there is no sense of being drawn, no directing influence is felt, conviction can give place not just to doubt but to active scepticism, and life may seem futile, cruel, and overwhelming. Most of one's life, no doubt, is spent in the unexciting middle zone, neither powerfully drawn nor totally desolate. But to be a Christian means that, whatever one's state, the journey goes on. It is staking everything on the belief that this way of using our one and only life will in the end be validated not only as the best for our human condition but as most truly in accord with ultimate reality.

One characteristic note of Christian life, therefore, is personal commitment, but also, and indeed for that very reason, commitment to truth. The quest for truth, for an awareness and understanding of the way things actually are, is vital to the human race, if only because in the end man cannot develop or even survive without it. Moreover, because human beings are complex creatures who live on many levels at once, a concern for truth cannot be confined to purely 'practical' matters. We cannot say, for instance, that realism is vital in science or technology, but that in questions of philosophy or religion we may believe anything we find helpful. There are people who can live at all only by escaping into a fantasy-world; but we rightly regard this as falling short of the best that a man or woman can be. The first and fundamental loyalty of the Christian conscience, therefore, must be to truth, the truth about God and the universe and the relation between them. A faith which ignores or distorts the realities of life is not worth having.

This means that one very important aspect of the Christian journey is a continuing intellectual effort after honest belief capable of throwing light on existence in all its complexity. This is an arduous if exciting adventure, one that has been carried on through each generation and that has drawn on all kinds of knowledge. At its best it is a corporate activity, something to which all Christians contribute, not just the clergy, or theologians in the narrow sense. (Every man, woman, or child who thinks about God at all engages in theology—a point that needs to be remembered by those who superficially decry that subject as the enclosed garden of remote academics. Theology is not undesirable, it is unavoidable. What matters is that it should be good theology.) What is more, this is an activity in which progress is possible. New knowledge and more thorough reflection can build on the achievement of the past to give us a fuller understanding of God. But such progress is never automatic. Much of the history of theology has been characterized by forgetting as well as by learning, with the result that instead of an accumulation of knowledge and understanding we see only the replacement of one partial insight by another equally partial.

To say this, however, is at once to raise an extremely complex issue, the discussion of which forms the very heart of this report. How do knowledge and understanding of God 'accumulate'? How do we genuinely enter into an inheritance of Christian insight without perverting our own quest for truth into a search for evidence and arguments to justify predetermined conclusions? In many fields this would be a bogus question, the implied conflict unreal. In history or philosophy or social and political studies, for example, it is by freely debating the questions treated by the great thinkers of the past, reframing them where necessary, and feeding in ideas and information new since their time, that we test their insights and make their wisdom our own. But the ultimate verdict on their work rests with us. We would be very foolish to think that there was little to be learned from them, or to treat them with contempt simply because they are of the past. But equally we are not expected to begin by assuming that they are right. In the Christian tradition, however, the inheritance of the past is most often described in terms which seem to call in question any right to speak, as we have been doing, of a 'journey', a 'quest', a 'voyage of discovery'. It is seen primarily not as man's search for God but as God's self-revelation to men; and this inevitably gives to the words which have been handed down an authoritative character, calling not so much for testing in the light of 'loyalty to truth' as for a response of humble acceptance in face of a truth already tested.

It is not all words in the immense library of Christian tradition on which this character is conferred. Different groups of Christians have their differing confessional documents and their preferred theologians. But the overwhelming majority of Christians agree in placing the Bible in a unique position of authority, and most would add to this, either as an explication or a definition of the biblical message, the two great creeds, the 'Apostles'' and the Nicene. It is in the handling of these texts, the Bible and the creeds, that the problem we have to consider comes to a head.

Before anything can usefully be said on these particular topics, however, there are certain background questions which must be examined. There is the whole matter of a proper attitude to the past: what are the real difficulties in the way of being receptive to the past? What are the advantages and dangers which the attempt to establish conscious contact with the past holds for us? There are the issues raised by our use of language: to what extent is 'religious' language special? How is it properly to be understood? These, put very briefly, are the subjects of the preliminary Sections 2 and 3. Section 4 then turns to our understanding and use of the Bible, Section 5 to that of the creeds.

In all this we have tried to do three things. First, to describe as honestly and accurately as we can some of the main difficulties which arise for Christians in this field at the present time, and to say why they arise. Secondly, to bring to the awareness of Christians a most important fact that is by and large overlooked: namely, that divergences in the way belief is expressed conceptually are to be expected from the very nature of Christian truth itself, and have in fact characterized the Church from New Testament times onwards. Thirdly, to show that underlying even very widely differing presentations of Christian faith there is in fact a common pattern or method of thinking, varying certainly in emphasis from one case to another but concerned in the last analysis with the same ingredients; and to suggest that the vital requirement for Christians today is not to force themselves to superficially agreed conclusions but to operate within the pattern—that is, to use in whatever way or proportion integrity allows the resources which the Christian community makes available.

2

The Pastness of the Past

People at large, in their attitude to the past, tend to fall into one or other of two categories; and in their feelings about the Christian past, Christians are no exceptions to this general rule. For some Christians the past comes mainly as something of a burden. The Church seems to have so much past, to cling on to it, to parade it, to make it more important than the present. Even today, when liturgical reform goes on apace, appropriation of the past and loyalty to it appear to be the prime concern in public worship. It is the ancient scriptures which are read and expounded, to the exclusion of more recent Christian writing. It is in the words of ancient creeds that we are expected to make our corporate profession of faith, in the songs of bygone ages that for the most part we are asked to voice the deepest feelings of our hearts. The sermon must often contain a brief historical lecture or other antiquarian material in order to pass from some biblical text to a contemporary point. Even our new services are discussed and criticized from the standpoint of their fidelity to a traditional pattern. Add to all this the antiquity of so many church buildings, or of the music and the art-work, and it is hardly surprising that some Christians find the past bearing down like a dark and oppressing cloud on the spirit.

Other Christians, however, react quite differently to this inheritance. For them what is ancient, be it in art, architecture, music, language, ritual, or institutions, is by that very fact more numinous, and so a more effective communication of God. Moreover, that the scriptures read and expounded publicly or meditated upon in private, the creeds and hymns in which the faith is proclaimed and celebrated, the sacred actions in which all Christians take part, are the very same as have been used for centuries, in some cases indeed by the first disciples of all, is to them the richest of all sources of pride, joy, and inspiration. To them, to be a Christian means precisely to belong to this age-old tradition, and they hold emphatically with G. K. Chesterton that 'a man cut off from his past . . . is a man most unjustly disinherited'.

These two types of response to the past are by no means peculiar to the realm of religion, though the conservatism which has been observed to be a characteristic of all great religions undoubtedly strengthens the second type in that context. They are a typically human phenomenon, to be found in societies of every kind, secular as well as sacred, and both would generally be considered necessary to the health and viability of any community. Nor do the two categories correspond exactly to the two sides of the so-called 'generation gap', even though there may normally be more young people who tend to respond in the first way and more older people in the second. The attitudes of any given individual in this matter are shaped by many different factors of temperament and upbringing, and by the prevailing culture. What is important for our present discussion is that this very obvious feature of human society should be borne in mind as we come to grips with certain new problems about man's relations to the past, of which thinking people have become fully aware only in recent times, and which are felt by many to have created something of a crisis for Christian belief in particular.

It will be best to begin by attempting to set out what we may call the negative side of the argument, the reasons why to many there does seem today to be a quite unprecedented challenge in this field which Christians must face.

The source of fundamental unease which these reasons seek to articulate is a feeling that, even though the past is so intensively obtruded on our notice, it may none the less be ultimately inaccessible. There is always some problem of communication between human beings; but communication with the past has problems all its own. If these cannot be overcome, then the past can hardly be used as an authentic resource for contemporary life.

Human beings communicate with one another in many different ways: by gestures; by plastic and pictorial forms—abstract or stereotyped or representational; symbols and conventional signs; objects of art and architecture; music; mathematical and other non-verbal systems; and, of course, by words. The material conveyed by these various means may also be highly diverse: factual statements, value-judgements, wishes, feelings, archetypal imagery, myths, metaphysical propositions, and so on. The effectiveness with which any means of communication transmits such material depends to a high degree on the existence of a context familiar to all parties. The same gesture may express opposite meanings or feelings in different societies. Without detailed guidance the art or music of another culture may easily be a closed book to us.

Words, however, sometimes seem to be in a different category. We have the feeling that they transcend these limitations more successfully than most other means of communication. This is true to a significant degree, but can be exaggerated. Words can be misinterpreted or even meaningless, simply because the situation in which they were uttered is not known. There are the obvious losses in translation from one language to another. The impact, say, of a poem may be totally changed because the original metaphysical setting is a blank to the reader.

Of all the barriers between ourselves and the words of another human being time can be one of the most important. In the case of a contemporary culture, however alien, we can, given patience, humility, and mutual good will, hope in time to learn and at least in imagination share some of its attitudes and assumptions. Those who are prepared to spend years living, for example, among Africans do, provided they are receptive and observant, acquire the gift of seeing many things with African eyes. But in our efforts to interpret the relics of the past we have no such recourse. The whole living world of which this work of art, that literary text, is a precipitate, has to be reconstructed before these things can be properly understood, and our only materials for the recon-struction are the art and the literature themselves. In the case even of so relatively recent a thing, and that from our own civilization, as a play of Shakespeare the most experienced critics can differ violently as to the tone of voice in which a particular passage is meant to be read, or the im-portance to be attached to, let us say, an expression of Christian belief; and such questions are often unanswerable, simply because we have never stood in the inner spiritual landscape of the men and women of that generation. When, therefore, we go back all the way to the ancient world, and ask ourselves what this or that text meant to the people of that society, no wonder we are baffled again and again. What did the myths of the gods and primeval heroes, of the origins of the world and of man really express? We trace the origins of European drama back to the Greeks, and still perform some of their greatest works; but what kind of purgation by pity and terror did the ordinary Athenian citizen undergo as he watched the first performance of the *Agamemnon* of Aeschylus? The scholarly literature of this century contains millions of words on the myths of Mesopotamia and ancient Egypt; but what the priests or public reciters felt or believed as they declaimed the *Epic of Creation*, or the crowds as they listened to it, we really have little or no idea. Experts argue about the nature and function of myth, but their conclusions do little to enable us to enrich our own lives from these magnificent but alien productions of long-dead genius. It is, generally speaking, only when they touch on the unchanging experiences of ordinary human life, when Gilgamesh is bereaved of his friend, or Euripides' Electra contemplates the misery of her wasted womanhood, that we feel truly at one with them across the ages.

Such questions are highly relevant to the Christian since his own sacred scriptures come from that ancient world. Most of the Old Testament, for example, is earlier than the high noon of Greek civilization. But even the New Testament sets many problems of a similar kind. Can we today genuinely share the thoughts and feelings of the first readers of St Paul's Epistles as they were urged to see in the events of the gospel their own liberation from the total determination of their lives by astral or planetary powers? Can we even begin to enter into the spiritual experience of a first-century Jew whose imagination was fired by detailed visions of an imminent apocalyptic end to the existing created order? And if we cannot, can we really be sure that we are understanding even the words of Jesus in the Gospels in the spirit in which they were originally intended? Nor, of course, is this kind of problem confined to words. It applies also to gestures. Does the ritual of baptism, for instance, still effectively express all the meaning once attached to it? To many the running commentary provided in the baptism service in the Book of Common Prayer has long seemed not only difficult in itself but also only artificially related to the action proceeding before their eyes. Yet it is reasonable to assume that to a world familiar with the mystery religions St Paul's account of baptism as a dying and rising again with Christ fitted naturally enough into their world-view.

This whole difficulty of standing alongside the men and women of the past and of understanding what they say by entering at least in imagination into the whole world of thought and feeling in which they say it is the really fundamental problem in creating a living relation with the past—far more fundamental than the more generally recognized one of what to do with ideas from the past which we now see to be mistaken. It is easy enough to see that the cosmology of the ancient world, for example, was scientifically incorrect. What is not so easy is to decide whether religious beliefs to which a finite, 'three-decker' universe seems to be integral have simply to be jettisoned, or whether there is in them some essential truth which can genuinely be transplanted into our own totally different cosmos. In any case, even assuming that we could by scholarly research rediscover the original thought-world of our inheritance, and enter into its primal meaning, would not the end-product be an antiquarian reconstruction, of interest only to the highly educated and intellectual, and in no sense a living, saving gospel for the poor and humble of our own day?

It might seem that we could slash through this Gordian knot. Why not do as the Church indeed did for many centuries, and simply treat the words not as clues to a long-gone and now irrelevant world of thought and feeling, but in effect as if we ourselves had uttered them? Then we need not bother what sacrifice, let us say, or kingship, or heaven and hell meant to the ancients. They could be fitted together in a coherent scheme of our own making, and mean what we could honestly take them to mean—symbolically, metaphorically, literally. But here we come up against precisely what is the new element in our present situation. Our ancestors treated the texts in this way because they did believe that the similarities between the various ages of human history far outweighed any differences. Superficially there had been changes, fundamentally men were the same. And this was plausible because until the sixteenth century the world-view of European man was indeed basically the same as that of the ancient cultures. The shattering changes in the understanding of reality that have marked the modern world have forced us to face the fact that man is an historical being, that he exists in a continuum of change, and that he cannot therefore take for granted that all ages and cultures shared his own principles and forms of thought.

If, then, we cannot with integrity treat the words of the past as though they were our own; and if at the same time the exercise of entering sympathetically into an understanding of the past is both problematic and productive of little that is of general value; what is our attitude to the past to be? We may acknowledge that it is the past which still surrounds us and weighs upon us with its words and monuments that has put us where we are; but the only form in which that past is relevant to life here and now is in its end-product, the present situation. Man must make his decisions—political, social, cultural, moral, religious—pragmatically in the light of the way things are. It is not that the wisdom of the past is to be despised or rejected. The real problem is to know in any serious sense what that wisdom was. Given such an appraisal of the situation, the natural results in a Christian context are: first, an emphasis on the contemporary community as the place where God's mind and will are to be encountered; secondly, a view of Christianity as an ongoing enterprise which inevitably changes its outward character from generation to generation by the dynamic of an indwelling Spirit; and thirdly, a diminution of emphasis on the formulas of the past, even of the biblical past. Jesus himself lives in the world of today not so much in his recorded words and actions as through the community which he founded but which may both in its teaching and manner of life have changed radically from anything he envisaged.

This, then, is one side of the argument. But another, very different reading of the situation is possible, and to this we must now turn.

First and fundamentally, it can be argued, the pastness of the past is the one thing which makes revelation possible. Whatever problems there may be in understanding or drawing upon the past, it has the one vital characteristic that it has happened and cannot be altered. It is not, as the present is, in a state of potentiality and flux. It has said its say, created its gestures, institutions, and memorials; and therefore what it bequeaths, so long as this is preserved at all, remains intrinsically the same. There is a givenness, an objective quality about the legacy of the past; and this comes through even in the subjective appropriations of the past by successive generations. If then we wish to think of a particular event or complex of events at some one stage in history as the vehicle of a decisive and unique revelation of God, then the pastness of the past, whatever the difficulties it may bring in its train, is absolutely necessary for our own good, since this alone makes certain data available in a constant form.

Secondly, are not the difficulties of communication with the past perhaps exaggerated by an age which, to its credit certainly, has discovered real and profound problems connected with history and culture, and is inclined to overplay them in consequence? In particular, our forefathers were human beings like ourselves, who had to live, as we do, with the permanent basic realities of human life and death, contingency and dependence; and there is no reason to assume that their feelings and reactions are all going to be opaque to us, or that, when they say something which we can imagine ourselves saying in a similar predicament, the sympathy is purely illusory.

Thirdly, it is generally agreed that straightforward statements of fact are not affected by these temporal and cultural barriers. So far as the Christian religion is concerned, some of its most important affirmations are of this kind: for example, that Jesus was born, crucified under Pontius Pilate, suffered, and was buried. The New Testament contains a great deal of material of this type; and while there is indeed argument about its historicity and the way in which it is to be evaluated against a rather sketchy background, the meaning of the words is in most cases clear enough. The same applies, as many non-Christians would testify, to much of the moral teaching both in the Old Testament and in the New.

Fourthly, we do in other disciplines accept the accumulated knowledge of the past as a basis for our own work. The scientific community does not do all the experiments over again. But even when we move into the more problematic area of the spiritual and moral life, we are by no means obliged to take the line that the past must measure up to the standards of this age, that we are in the main right, and that anything which cannot be fitted into our own patterns of thought and behaviour must be rejected. It is at least equally serious and reasonable to allow the past to act as a critique of ourselves, and to change our own most cherished notions of what is right or possible in the light of an older and greater wisdom. The same sort of choice can apply in non-verbal fields. If unleavened bread and wine are no longer everyday food—and in many countries they are highly exotic—one possible view is that the Eucharist has ceased to be what it originally was, the use of a cultural datum as the vehicle of spiritual truth, and that the elements should be changed. But another possible view is that to do this would be to sever the explicit link with an historical event of paramount importance; and that exoticism achieves precisely the point of stressing that a saving and revelatory act took place in the past. For those who put the emphasis on this aspect, the adventure of Christian thought and belief will be much more a matter of going to school with the past, and of allowing the gospel to open one's eyes to see existence in a new way. For such people the Bible and the creeds in particular will have priority over their own reflections, and the work of the indwelling Spirit of God will be to unpack, develop, and make real to us the creative word of God in Jesus.

The truth in any or all of these various arguments can be usefully assessed only when we come to consider in more concrete detail the actual character of the Christian past as embodied in the Bible and the creeds. But one point can be made straightaway. Our new-found consciousness of man as an historical being can never be purely negative in its implications. If it makes us aware of the difficulty of entering into the world of thought and feeling of the past, it has also awakened us more sharply to the degree in which even our most 'modern' characteristics are conditioned by the past. But if the latter is a judgement we can validly make, then it is quite impossible to adopt an attitude of total agnosticism towards the past. We do know something not just about our present inheritance but also about those who bequeathed it to us; and one of the ways in which we learn to make the best of our present resources is by understanding and evaluating the continuing process from which they derive. For the Christian community, then, as for any other, a responsible attitude to the present involves a sympathetic effort to understand the past and a serious dialogue with it.

It will be apparent, however, from what has been said in this section that the major question at issue between the two general approaches we have described is the extent to which such understanding and dialogue is practicable. This question can hardly be discussed seriously without some preliminary consideration of the nature of religious language, both our own and that of the past; and it is this topic that we must consider.

3
The Nature of Religious Language

For most of us, living our ordinary day-to-day lives, the ideal use of language could probably be summed up in the phrase, 'I say what I mean, and I mean what I say'. When we are unable to say what we mean, when we find ourselves 'at a loss for words', as we put it, we feel frustrated and vaguely inadequate. 'I know what I mean, but I can't quite describe it', we say, and either go on getting it wrong, knowing we are getting it wrong, or lapse into baffled silence. Sometimes this defeat is due, of course, to lack of vocabulary or to our not being clear to start with what it is we really want to say. We have failed to observe or think clearly enough before speaking. But at other times there is a more profound reason for our breakdown. We are trying to convey the nature of some deep feeling or of some experience that has greatly moved us, and we just know that the task is impossible. If we are of an imaginative turn of mind, we may try to give some idea of our experience by comparisons—'It was rather like so-and-so.' But we know that this is only the roughest of indications, and that even a whole series of such examples cannot hope to do more than mark out a kind of wide circle round the target area. But the fact that we cannot describe the experience does not make us doubt the reality either of what it was we saw or heard or encountered in some indefinable way or of our own feelings in response to it. Quite the contrary: the event in question was probably one of the most 'real' things in our whole life.

It is as well to start from this after all very commonplace fact of life in order to remind ourselves that there is no reason to be suspicious when we are told that language about God or about religious experience cannot adequately describe the realities to which it claims to refer. There is nothing singular about this. Words are very far from being the all-sufficient instruments we like to think them, a truth of which we have proof every day. But in the case of language about God and his dealings with the world there is a built-in reason why this is true not just in some instances but all the time. If God is truly to be what we want the word 'God' to mean, then he must be beyond adequate expression. 'If you have grasped it, it is not God', wrote St Augustine. Nevertheless, no more than with our ordinary 'ineffable' experiences does this mean that God is unreal or that nothing can be said which will at any rate point our minds in his direction.

There is perhaps a further insight to be gained from our everyday example. If we are trying to convey the character of some very real and profound but elusive experience, then we are much more likely to succeed with someone whose life and temperament have made them in tune with us, an intimate friend or a genuinely close relative or marriage partner, for example, than with someone unsympathetic or whose life has been spent in totally different circumstances and pursuits. The person close to us can often pick up what we are trying to say from the most inadequate clues, and their own experiences tend to be more of the kind that direct them to an intuitive recognition of our own. Much the same can be said of religious language. Religious language, precisely because it cannot help being an attempt to indicate the ultimately indescribable, communicates much more effectively within the community of believers than to those outside. In its richest forms it is the language of a community, and articulates the most intimate and profound aspects of its common life. This is not to say that there can be no communication with those outside, any more than it would be true to say that we can never share our everyday elusive experiences with a stranger; for logically, if communication beyond the limits of the community were impossible, no one new would ever come to share its experience, and the community would die out. But communication with a stranger does normally call for more 'translation' and 'unpacking', and can only rarely hope to convey the fullness of that to which the words in question refer. Anyone who has ever done evangelistic work will know the truth of this.

Furthermore, words have overtones. Outside the driest of technical documents there is probably no such thing as an absolutely bare statement. The most ordinary remark made in the home will normally operate on at least three levels, to convey, let us hope, information, affection, and approval, not by using separate words for each function but by expressing all of them at once in something as simple as 'Breakfast is ready'. So too it is with religious language. When St Thomas Aquinas writes: 'The most appropriate name for God is HE WHO IS', then at one level this is just a statement in metaphysics. But to anyone within the community of faith the words are also a voicing of love (since 'name' is both a term in logic and also an expression of relationship, and to care about finding the most appropriate name is an act of love), and of praise and adoration (since self-existent being is beyond telling greater than we), and of awe, wonder, and humility (since to say this about God is to confess that his inmost nature is far beyond our comprehension).

Paradoxically, then, such a statement carries with it a kind of footnote: 'Precisely because this is true, it is also wholly inadequate.' This again has its adumbration in everyday experience. It is only a very conceited or superficial person who says of another human being, 'Oh yes, I understand him perfectly.' By contrast the characteristic utterance of love is 'No, it's no good; I can't begin to tell you'. Any attempt to provide a complete rundown on someone else's personality, as in writing a character reference, is always in the end a failure; and never more so than when we think we have succeeded. If any such description is treated as definitive, then in that moment it becomes a lie. And if this is true of our words about other human beings, how much more true will it be of what we say about God!

But equally, just as we would be very angry if it was suggested that because we could not do justice to our friends therefore we could say nothing about them at all, or that whatever we did say was altogether wrong, so the religious believer, for all his disclaimers about the inadequacy of his statements, is quite clear that they do say something worth saying. Towards the end of his life St Thomas Aquinas, we are told, remarked to his friend, Friar Reginald, that he had seen things which made all his writings 'like straw'; but he did not therefore conclude that they were false and ought to be withdrawn from circulation. The plain fact is that men do speak about God; and thus there is an air of unreality, to say the least, in asking whether such an activity is possible. What matters is to understand how we speak about God, what are our limitations when we do so, and how we can speak most truly and effectively.

First of all, then, we need to establish the general principle, already hinted at more than once, that God is far beyond the compass of any words we can use of him. This principle operates in two ways. On the one hand, because God is fundamentally unlike any other being, we frequently have to insist that he is 'not this' or 'not that'. He is *in*finite, *im*mortal, *in*effable; his existence is underived, not subject to contingency. Or, in the more poetic language of the Second Isaiah: 'To whom will you liken God?' and again, 'For my thoughts are not your thoughts, neither are your ways my ways, says the Lord' (Isa. 40.18; 55.8). These negative statements are of great importance, because they prevent us from forming false ideas or from looking in the wrong direction when we think about God. Instead they point us in the direction of the transcendent, where silent adoration is the only fitting response, not the chatter of our feeble intellect. On the other hand, because positive statements about God are not only legitimate but essential (for how otherwise could we know how to live our lives in a right relationship with him?), this principle has a wider application. It tell us that we must never make an idol of any of our ideas about God, never think of him exclusively in terms of one earthly image. In short, our general rule must be this: there are some things which we can affirm that God is *not*; and there are many other things which we can affirm that he *is*, but only in a way that exceeds our affirmation, and never exclusively.

This brings us to our second point: since we can and must make positive statements about God, how are we to understand them? In speaking about him we have to take words which refer primarily to earthly realities. The Bible is full of them: King, Father, Judge, Redeemer, Saviour, Husband, Shepherd, and so forth. But obviously none of these can be applied straight, in their literal human sense. Even a word like 'Creator', which to many may seem predominantly a religious term, is only an image derived from human experience, and has to be heavily qualified when applied to God, in order to make clear that it cannot be used of him purely in the way we use it of human creativity. Our images then are models. The human realities to which they ordinarily refer reflect in a limited and earthly way something that is in an eternal and unique manner true of God. If we are to use any model properly, we have to be aware of the ways in which the earthly reality does or does not apply. This, for example, is one thing that the Fourth Gospel is doing in the discourse on Jesus as the Good Shepherd in John 10—taking a traditional image of God, and showing in what ways it can and cannot legitimately be used as a model. Similarly, we have to remember constantly that all the models qualify each other. Hence the importance of keeping them all in use, and never allowing our vision of God or our understanding of his relationship to the world to be narrowed down, so that we contemplate him only through the medium of one or two of them:

> Our little systems have their day;
>   They have their day, and cease to be.
>   They are but broken lights of Thee,
> And Thou, O Lord, art more than they.

But these images—all images, no doubt, but especially those of the Bible—are more than just concepts, to be apprehended by the analytic intellect alone. Just as we saw that even the simplest words can operate on many levels at once—informative, emotive, evaluative—so images touch the whole personality down to the very deepest levels of the psyche, and can and should, where appropriate, involve our bodily life as well. Religious language customarily comes to us in a context of actions loaded with significance; and we receive its meaning not just mentally but sacramentally. At the very heart of Christian worship is the classic example of this, the Eucharist. The meaning of the image, 'the Bread of God which comes down from heaven', is by no means exhausted in the act of Holy Communion; far from it. But the physical reception of the elements is one vital means by which our whole self is placed in thankful dependence on God as the one true source of life, and the image exerts its full effect. The images of religious language are also symbols of a larger non-verbal reality, and come fully alive only where that total reality is involved in our openness to the truths which they mediate. It is precisely because of this quality that religious language can exercise a unifying and healing influence on the whole personality, and act, in traditional Christian terminology, as a 'means of grace'.

It will be clear from what has been said so far that one of the principal difficulties in dealing with religious language is to find some coherent logical approach to our positive statements about God. If we apply words to God in their ordinary literal or univocal sense, then we all too easily make God in our own image and fall into idolatry; if we use them in an entirely different or equivocal sense, then we have no reason for using one word rather than another, and we are lost in agnosticism. One method of handling this problem which has a real if limited usefulness is that which applies the principle of analogy to what we say about God. Our ideas are based on the perfections and excellences we can see in God's finite creatures. It is because these are real perfections and excellences, reflecting and communicating something of the goodness and nature of God, that God is known to us at all. But in order to be able to apply these visible perfections to God, we must first remove from them all that belongs to them only in virtue of their finitude and creaturehood; and then the concept thus purified must be raised to infinity to be applicable to God. Knowledge, for example, is such an excellence. But in us, knowledge is fitful, discursive, and dependent on sense. When these limitations, incidental to knowledge in our finite existence, are removed from the idea of knowledge, this can then be heightened to convey a clearer mental concept of what the all-embracing, direct, intuitive, and creative knowledge possessed by God might be. This analogical treatment of language about God, though applicable only to abstract concepts, can provide a useful logical check against saying either too little or too much.

It is often loosely remarked nowadays that religious language is 'poetic'. This a word which can be used so vaguely in this context that it serves no useful purpose and may even be seriously misleading. It would certainly be quite disastrous in its effects (and incidentally untrue to the nature of the greatest poetry) if it were used to suggest that religious beliefs need have no definite content, and that, whatever the surface meaning of the words, any interpretation, however arbitrary, is valid so long as it commends itself to the individual spiritual judgement. To say that all religious language is inadequate, or that we are dealing with images and symbols of a transcendent and ultimately inexpressible reality, does not mean that 'anything goes'. It is true that our models, even when carefully qualified and used to correct and complement each other, still are only pointers; but they do point in certain directions and not in others. We may not be able to grasp all that they include, but we do know that there are quite a lot of things which they exclude. Moreover, in a faith like Christianity which seeks to wrestle with the ultimate significance of certain specific historical events, in particular those connected with Jesus, some of its central religious statements will always have to be taken in a straightforward referential sense. Thus, whatever their other implications, the words, 'suffered under Pontius Pilate, was crucified, dead, and buried', must first be held to be true in the natural sense which they would have if used of any human being. Perhaps there are very few statements in Christianity of which it can be said that their significance is exhausted by their 'literal' meaning; but there are a number of cases where it plays an important role in determining whether interpretations at some other level are valid interpretations or not. The resurrection of Jesus is such a case, where the principle applies in a way that is at once extremely complex and also of very special importance. Most Christians on reflection would probably agree that the affirmation that Jesus was dead and is alive cannot adequately be understood merely in a bare, 'literal' sense—indeed that there could be no form of words expressing this idea which was purely literal. Yet, unless any suggested interpretation sees the original intention of the biblical and credal language as at any rate one trustworthy pointer to the full truth, it is hard to see how it can properly be regarded as an interpretation of the earlier affirmation at all.

It is against the background of the general considerations sketched out in this section that we must now examine the questions posed for Christian belief today by those basic items in our inheritance, the Bible and the creeds.

4

The Christian and the Bible

A preliminary but vital fact to bear in mind—it has often been pointed out before, but still needs to be repeated—is that the Bible is not a single book but an immensely varied collection of writings. We are used to hearing the Bible spoken of as one in a list of literary masterpieces, such as Homer, Dante, or Shakespeare, and so we tend to think of it as homogeneous in the same way. Again, for many generations the magnificent but uniform style of the Authorized Version has made the various elements in the Bible seem much more alike than they really are; and their diversity is only now becoming more apparent with the help of modern translations. But the documents in the Bible cover a time-span of some twelve or thirteen centuries. They are written in three different languages. The contents include legends, historical narrative, poetry both secular and sacred, civil and religious laws, ritual prescriptions, proverbial wisdom, speculative theology, prophecy, folk-tales, moral and ethical instruction, letters, records of visions and dreams, and some material for which any classification is virtually impossible, such as the Gospels, which are a unique form of literature. The greater part of this material reflects ancient Jewish culture, but this was continuously receptive of influences from other societies, such as Egypt, Mesopotamia, Persia, and Greece. In the New Testament we find in addition the impact of the morals, religion, philosophy, and social conditions of the hellenistic world of the early Roman Empire.

The Bible, therefore, does not come just from 'the past', but from many different 'pasts', some of which were already so unfamiliar even in biblical times that they were plainly misunderstood by other biblical writers. Nevertheless, there is one fact which gives all this material at least a common external frame of reference. The Bible contains not only the earliest surviving records of Christianity itself but also an extensive sample of the historical process within which Christianity emerged. The principal reality in the background of Christianity is Israel; and in the Old Testament the life of Israel is documented over a longer period and from more aspects than that of any other ancient society. There are gaps—some quite lengthy periods of time and many facets of ordinary life—which are thinly covered or not at all; and on the crucial generations immediately leading to the time of Jesus the Old Testament tells us nothing and even the Apocrypha very little. But when every qualification has been made, it is still true that the Old Testament is an essential source-book without which many things in the New Testament would be totally incomprehensible to us.

This brings us to another unifying factor within the Bible as a whole. For Christians of the New Testament period their 'Bible' was the Old Testament in virtually its present form; and the fundamental reason for this was their conviction that the God who had saved them through Jesus was the God of Israel of whom the Old Testament spoke and by whose spirit its writers had been inspired. Hence most of the arguments in the New Testament made use of the Old to support and clinch their points. Even the resurrection of Jesus could be validated as an act of God because, as the first Christians believed, it had been foretold in the scriptures. And in controversy with the Jews it is the correct interpretation of these scriptures which is of crucial importance, precisely because both parties accepted them as of divine inspiration.

Whether Jesus himself shared quite such a rigorous standpoint on the inspired character of the Old Testament is much debated. Certainly Galilee was regarded by the orthodox of Jerusalem as sitting loose to the full observance of the Law; and in the Gospels Jesus is presented as overruling for humanitarian reasons at any rate certain current decisions on what the Law implied. On the other hand, in one well-supported tradition of his teaching about divorce he adopts a stricter standard than the Mosaic law, basing himself on a phrase in the creation story of Genesis 2. Such relatively minor variations, however, do not necessarily imply more than that Jesus operated within a general contemporary framework of teaching by means of scriptural exposition, but that some of his personal interpretations of Scripture were controversial. Far more radical questions are opened up by other material in the Gospels; for example, the contrast in the Sermon on the Mount between 'It was said by the ancients' and 'I say to you'; his use of arguments from the facts of everyday life to establish truths about God and to controvert current notions, as in the saying about God making the sun shine and the rain fall on evil and good men alike; and his highly individual use of parables to convey his own creative insights into the nature of God's sovereignty and fatherly providence. It is related that his teaching struck his hearers by its quality of personal authority as opposed to the scribal method, which presumably meant the exegesis of

Scripture and tradition. The Fourth Gospel reflects a similar tradition in its picture of Jesus bringing a direct revelation from the Father, surpassing and superseding that of the Old Testament.

Nevertheless, whatever Jesus' attitude to Scripture may have been, the tradition of his life and teaching was itself in the end canonized as sacred Scripture. The outcome of that canonization was that, even if Jesus may himself have handled scriptural material very freely or even criticized it, it became quite unthinkable for Christians to act in that way now that Jesus' own final and supreme revelation of God was fixed for all time on the written page. The prime objective now was to prove that the whole Bible, the Old Testament, the Gospels, and the apostolic writings, was internally consistent, and that the same truths, plain in the New Testament, hidden in the Old, were present throughout to the discerning eye. By the third century almost every book in the canon had been laid under contribution. The methods employed were those which every cultural tradition of that age, Christian, Jewish, or pagan, applied to its venerated ancient writings. The actual words on the page, with little or no regard for context, were what mattered. The task of the exegete was to open the reader's eyes to the underlying meanings disguised from him in allegorical language. On this basis any phrase might prove as valuable as any other; for all enshrined, could one but see how, the same fundamental verities, whether these were the truths of Platonism in Homer or of the Christian gospel in Leviticus.

The effect of this approach was to put all Scripture on a single level of inspiration. Every letter of the sacred text was what it was for some purpose. From this point of view crude or cruel elements, sordid stories, anything which (as we would say) presented a 'sub-Christian' view of God, need no longer be a problem. Anything odd or shocking was, so to say, a warning light to alert the reader to the presence of hidden truth. But the truth so hidden was very far from odd or shocking. It had to turn out in the end to be some aspect of the mainstream faith of the Christian Church; and any theologian, such as Origen, who made the text say something different was to be condemned. The whole Bible, first the Old and then the New Testament, was thus effectively converted into a handbook of Christian doctrine.

With the Reformation came a strong reaction against such allegorizing interpretation, and an insistence on the plain sense of the words as the vehicle of any spiritual meaning the biblical author may have intended. The influence of the humanist studies of the Renaissance was powerful, and operated in two main ways. First, commentators began to devote themselves to questions of textual criticism and historical background. Secondly, many of them made use of a method deriving ultimately from Aristotle for extracting the essence of the scriptural message. This was to concentrate on what they regarded as the main topics treated by any scriptural writer, and to expound primarily the passages bearing on these—an approach which foreshadowed the 'biblical theology' movement of our own day, and gave a strongly doctrinal slant to biblical studies. Calvin, however, saw that this led to the neglect of much biblical material. For him the whole Bible was God speaking, though speaking in words adapted to the limitations of men. Hence the vital requirement was to study and understand every word in its plain signification. Any tensions or seeming contradictions that might result were simply the inevitable result of communicating the ineffable God to men, and must therefore be accepted and held in tension, in order that the whole truth about God might make its impact on men's lives.

During the last one hundred and fifty years, however, even this more realistic approach to the scriptures has in its turn proved insufficient. One result, as is well known, has been a widespread scepticism, dismissing the Bible as of little interest or relevance, save perhaps for a few outstanding passages; and this attitude is certainly not confined to non-Christians. Of other approaches, seeking to make full use of the biblical material yet without loss of intellectual integrity, two call for particular notice.

The first is that best characterized by its controlling concept of 'progressive revelation'. This approach starts from a recognition that the conception of God and of his will which we find at the end of the biblical story is richer and more complete, both morally and spiritually, than that which obtained at the beginning. Whether we see this as the result of God's education of man by a gradually increasing self-disclosure adapted to man's progress, or as the product of man's evolution in his quest for truth, the fact remains. From Joshua to Jesus is quite unquestionably an astonishing advance. The graph does not move upwards in a straight line; there are early peaks and later troughs. Nor is everything in the New Testament Church admirable and everything in the Israel of the Book of Judges outgrown. But progress there was, and any satisfactory treatment of Scripture must take account of this salient fact. The principal danger in this approach, if unqualified by other considerations, is that a concentration on the final achievement of the process mirrored in the Bible, and its use as a norm, can cause us to overlook much of importance along the way and to undervalue material less obviously compatible with our own contemporary ideal of Christianity. Also it has sometimes been a defect of this approach to depict the revelatory process as one simply of discovery through insight and reflection without reference to those experiences of encounter with the living, speaking God to which the biblical writers themselves repeatedly testify.

These limitations in the 'progressive revelation' approach were among the main factors which stimulated the second major attempt to find a modern solution to the question of the right place of the Bible in Christian belief. This was the movement known broadly as 'biblical theology'. This term does in fact cover two quite distinct enterprises. The first was descriptive in nature, and sought to identify and expound in contemporary language the theology or theologies which did historically underlie the Old Testament or the New or both together. The second was an exercise in normative theology, the endeavour to construct a doctrinal system or systems for Christianity legitimately derived from the biblical data. Both enterprises shared two important characteristics: they both proceeded on the expectation of finding material of real theological value today in any and every part of the Bible; and they were scrupulously concerned only to 'read out' of the texts those ideas that were really there, instead of reading into them, as earlier Christian centuries had done, beliefs formulated only long after the bulk of Scripture had been written.

There is no doubt that the many great exponents of biblical theology have achieved results for which Christians everywhere will long be grateful. One of the problems with which the Bible confronts the theologian is that relatively little of it is what we would call 'theology'. The theology of each of the various writers, schools, or traditions is for the most part unexpressed. It forms the assumptions which they bring to bear on existence, and which control their interpretation of it in relation to God, but which they only rarely describe. In showing, therefore, that the theologies underlying the Bible do belong to a single family, and share fundamental family resemblances, the biblical theology movement has brought to light a genuine community of witness in Scripture which makes talk of the 'unity of the Bible' more than an idle phrase, and does show, moreover, that this unity is in essence theological and not merely cultural. All this cannot but make the biblical insights more meaningful and more accessible to contemporary man.

But the question must be asked: does it do this only by making the Bible itself expendable? Granted that the exercise may be incomplete, the interpretations in part incorrect, nevertheless in principle may we not one day arrive at a point where we have got out of the Bible everything there is to get, and what is more, have succeeded in presenting this essential message in terms more useful to present-day people than those of the Bible itself? Is any one particular version of a piece of religious language indispensable? After all, we do not have even the words of Jesus as he uttered them, but only in translation at best. Might not a paraphrase of Paul be as good as Paul, and possibly better? In short, do we now need the Bible at all, except for the experts to check on the trustworthiness of the various contemporary presentations of it?

The torrent of popular and successful books over the last fifty years expounding the message and meaning of this or that part of the Bible suggests that such questions are not as silly as they may seem at first sight. For many people the experience of reading a book about the Bible has proved more helpful than reading the Bible itself, and has not necessarily encouraged them to go back to it. But there is one very good reason why we should not settle for a series of expositions of Scripture, brought up to date every generation, instead of the original texts. We need the Bible to confront us constantly with a two-sided fact: first, that diversity of understanding within an overall unity has from the beginning been the mark of God's people in their relationship with his truth; and secondly, that the unity has been apprehended as having its ultimate ground in the God whom men seek to understand. From this standpoint the diversity is both inevitable and itself a pointer to God in whom the unity is to be found.

The varied religious actuality of the Bible is all too easily lost beneath the smooth surface of systematic presentation in our own contemporary idiom. It may be that in this context there is a lesson to be learned from the theory of modern literary criticism. It is today generally agreed that there is no such thing as the one true 'meaning' of a work. A play of Shakespeare, an epic or lyric poem, a study of mankind in a great novel or historical work will all of them have many layers of facets of 'meaning' and the more of them, indeed, the greater the genius that inspired them. The aim of criticism, therefore, is not to extract the 'correct' interpretation but to enable the reader to find meaning in the work for himself. This is not to say that any meaning a reader chooses to see in a literary text is as good as any other. The difference between good and bad criticism is precisely that the light which bad criticism claims to throw on a work is in fact a false light, changing out of recognition the object it purports to illuminate. Good criticism brings out clusters or families of themes which a consensus of opinion will in time acknowledge as all of them valid interpretation. In dealing with a vast collection of varied material such as the Bible our first concern, therefore, should be to open ourselves to the depths of meaning in each individual document without worrying whether or how these are going to harmonize with the meanings of some other writer.

In fact something very similar to this happens within the Bible itself. In the latter part of the Old Testament period Jewish writers are already giving their own interpretations of earlier biblical texts; and the New Testament is full of varying treatments of the ancient scriptures. Nor is it only other writings which are handled so diversely. Both in the Old and New Testaments we find side by side strikingly different, if not absolutely incompatible, readings of events or types of common human situation.

To see some event as an 'act of God' is already to speak from the standpoint of faith. Such events are not necessarily labelled by signs and portents to alert men to what they are—a point which is already acknowledged in the Old Testament. If the Exodus from Egypt was accompanied by miracles, the sack of Jerusalem in the sixth century BC, the deportation of her citizens, and their eventual return were outwardly 'natural' events. Again, in the later Old Testament period there is a strong trend in certain schools of thought towards applying the lessons learned from the divine acts in earlier times to at least the main outlines of each individual life. But a conviction that the hand of God is at work in a particular set of circumstances is only the first step. Even where there is agreement on God's moral character, the interpretation of his purpose in these circumstances is still something about which agreement is far to seek. The Old Testament contains several very different understandings of the events of the sixth century; and as to the individual life, if calamity overtakes a man, is it because he is a sinner? Or is his loyalty being tested? Or is his character being improved by fatherly chastening? Or is he marked out as one of God's favoured 'poor', awaiting the final deliverance?

The greatest of all the 'acts of God' in the Bible, outstripping all the rest by far, is, of course, the life, death, and resurrection of Jesus. But even this is not unambiguously marked as divine—not even to the disciples until the first Easter; and even after that, many Jews who had rejected him before still refused to accept the truth of the gospel claim.

Nor among those who did accept it was there unanimity on its interpretation. Different accounts are given of the person of Jesus; different meanings are found in his achievement; different conclusions are drawn as to the probable consequences and the requirements involved for those who would be his disciples. These evaluations are not necessarily incompatible; many of them can coexist happily enough. But it would be idle to pretend that in some cases, as for example in the contrasting presentations of the person of Jesus in the Synoptists and in John, the differences are not profound.

In short, right from the very beginning of Christianity there is pluriformity in the faith,[1] just as there had been in the faith of Israel before it. Moreover, this pluriformity is no merely superficial feature, incidental to the underlying unity. Just as much as the unity it is ingrained, ineradicable, generated by the essential nature of biblical religion. For the Bible is not, like the Qur'an, the work of one man; nor is it, like the Buddhist scriptures, the elaboration of the thought of one man; nor has it, like the scriptures of Zoroastrianism, been subjected to one overriding dogmatic pattern. The Bible is the product of many individuals. Some of these were traditionalists, some radicals or sceptics; some found God's will in an ideal past, others could envisage it fully worked out only in a transformed future. Among its contributors we find men of power and victims of oppression; ecstatic visionaries and prosaic intellectuals; highly educated theologians and ordinary working people; members of a priestly caste and fierce opponents of institutionalized cult. These and other equally distinctive individuals wrestled with God, trying to fathom and express his dealings with men. To help them the men of the Old Testament had certain sacred traditions, their observation of life, and their experience of God himself through prayer and worship. The men of the New Testament had all these, but also and supremely 'the things concerning Jesus'. Out of these elements, in the fire of exultation or suffering, their words were forged. Their concern was to tell it as they saw it. In the process they were often polemical. They corrected or rewrote earlier histories; they denounced error with a violence of language that verged at times on the frenzied or the obscene. The New Testament is alive with controversy from end to end: Jesus' teaching and indeed his whole ministry are shaped by his clashes with the factions all around him; Paul is in endless argument with those who try to undermine his work; the letters of John hammer

1 For a more detailed treatment of this feature in the New Testament, cf. Appendix
  A: 'The Unity and Pluriformity of the New Testament'.

away at the dangers of false belief; and on every page of the whole corpus is evidence of the constant war which the earliest Church was forced to fight on two fronts, against Judaism and against Hellenism. How then could the Bible be anything else but a collection of many different insights, most of them passionately propounded, many of them inevitably in tension with one another? That is how, in the Bible, truth is communicated. If we do not like it, we can go elsewhere.

But, of course, we cannot go elsewhere, for there is nowhere else to go. Quite apart from anything else, the Gospels are absolutely indispensable because they are virtually our only source of knowledge about Jesus; and Christianity is founded on the assertion that God's redemptive activity is decisively revealed in 'the word which Jesus speaks and is'. The New Testament as a whole is, in essence, a series of attempts to convey the significance of this affirmation, attempts of such power and insight that they established themselves from a relatively early stage as uniquely authoritative. And, as we have seen already, where the New Testament goes, the Old Testament goes too.

Some would wish here to draw attention to the particular tradition of language and imagery which is to be found in the Old and New Testaments. This is itself diverse, like its content, yet recognizably a single tradition belonging to its age and locality. It is the precipitate of the experience of Israel and the New Testament Church, and at the same time the expression of it. The relation between language and reality is so intimate as to be virtually indissoluble. If this is so, then our access to the reality to which the scriptures, in all their variety of expression, bear witness has at some stage to be through these scriptures. That is why the exposition of Scripture continues to be important in the life of the Church, and why the elaboration of Christian theology, with its own developing language tradition, is continuously related to the interpretation of Scripture.

There is nothing, therefore, to be done about the Bible and its heterogeneous, dynamic character. We are stuck with it. What we can do something about is our attitude towards it. Until very recently the Christian reaction has been, as we saw earlier, to regard this diversity and tension, this dialectical presentation of truth, as somehow a defect which it was the Church's vocation to remedy by producing a coherent doctrinal synthesis out of the jostling biblical data. But a very different attitude is possible. Instead of deploring this character and trying to correct it, we might ask ourselves whether it may not be we who are wrong. Perhaps this is the way in which God is best communicated;

and perhaps we would do better to take the Bible as a pattern instead of a problem. It is, after all, a fact that the scriptures do still, even across astonishingly wide gulfs of time and culture, succeed in speaking to the minds and hearts of a great variety of people. One reason for this, even if Christians have only recently begun to appreciate it, may well be the pluriformity of the good news and the intensity which this makes possible.

Exposition of the Bible cannot, however, be dispensed with. For most people most of the time some degree of explanation, 'translation', illumination is necessary. Even if we read the Bible on our own, we are usually engaged in a somewhat similar process in our own heads in order to penetrate its meaning for us. But if we have fears about this, perhaps we can again learn from the Bible itself to exorcize them. It is perfectly true that no one expounds the Bible to himself or to anyone else without bringing to the task his own prior frame of reference, his own pattern of assumptions which derives from sources outside the Bible. If we ask whether this does not, as it were, contaminate the biblical revelation, the answer is quite simply that precisely the same thing happens within the New Testament itself. Such passages as the Prologue to the Fourth Gospel or the first chapter of Hebrews are striking examples of bringing a prefabricated conceptual framework to the interpretation of the 'things concerning Jesus'.

It was, no doubt, the very success of the New Testament writers which led to the misuse of their work. The original character of the individual writings was forgotten, and revelation came to be thought of as a static thing, delivered to men once for all in these sacred and inspired texts. The principal task of the Church was now to guard the deposit of faith, to hand on the sound teaching, and to drive out those who would corrupt it. The beginnings of this attitude are already to be found within the New Testament itself, in the Pastoral Epistles, and there is an emphasis here which, if Christianity is to have any coherent and continuing identity, needs to be retained. But as a method of getting the most out of the Bible, of treating it as a living creative resource for faith through all the changes of history, it leaves much to be desired.

For the New Testament itself handed on to the Church a volume of unfinished business. Within its pages we can see issues being shaped, ideas coming into being. The process could not, did not stop when the writer of 2 Peter, or whatever is the latest book in the canon, laid down his pen. The Bible is often not relevant to our problems because the precise questions to which it addresses itself are not those which we would wish put. But it did inaugurate a tradition within which those problems can be handled, and handled in a way that is in keeping with the spirit of the Bible. This surely is one major role of the Holy Spirit. Scripture has to be filled out by prayer and thought and the ongoing life and witness of the Church. The resources at our disposal are the Bible plus the use made of it in the Christian community down the ages.

The Bible is not an exhaustive compendium of spiritual wisdom nor a collection of rulings and definitions that can be automatically applied without error to any new situation. The miracle of the Bible is rather that it is inexhaustible; its creative power goes on stimulating new developments in tune with its own spirit. As in a gallery of family portraits, the same features reappear in generation after generation of men and women who nevertheless are of their own age. At the present time, for example, we see this spirit still at work in such new guises as the Latin-American 'theology of liberation' and in 'Black theology', which employ the biblical writings as aids to a dialogue with and illumination of their own existential situation.

To speak of the Bible as the 'Word of God', or the 'Word of God in the words of men', is just as much a judgement of faith as to speak of some historical event as an 'act of God'. It is not a proposition that can be proved. There are many Christians who wish to keep this language when talking of the Bible; there are others to whom it does not come easily. But no one who seriously intends to be a Christian can avoid wrestling with the Bible as part of that given tradition with which, if he would follow Jesus at all, he must come to terms. And when he does so, then, whatever his presuppositions, he finds there 'words of eternal life'.

5

The Christian and the Creeds

Of all the major world religions Christianity is the only one that has developed confessional formulas. Neither in the two other Semitic religions—Judaism and Islam—nor in the eastern faiths, such as Hinduism and Buddhism, is there anything that is strictly parallel with the creeds. The reason for this is, in part, to be found in the context within which the early Church developed. As it moved towards self-consciousness and an awareness of its identity, the Church had to differentiate itself from the Judaism within which it had arisen and from pagan thought with which it was coming into contact. The result was the progressive creation of standards of orthodoxy. However, the singularity of Christianity in this respect also arose from the historical fact that it was a special 'blend' of historical, metaphysical, and theological elements. The creeds were the outcome of the special historical status accorded to Jesus when interpreted partly in biblical categories and partly in terms of Graeco-Roman philosophy.

Since in Christianity the person of Jesus is central, the confessional formulas of the Christian link affirmations about Jesus and about his life, death, and resurrection, from which the religion took its rise, with the main tenets of Christian belief about God. And because 'faith', the act and state of believing, was from the start a primary feature of the Christian life and the way in which salvation was appropriated and retained, it is natural enough that the Christian creeds are not only statements of certain beliefs but also affirmations that the speaker himself believes.

Creeds in the general sense, and even in the particular literary form with which we are familiar, are therefore to be expected in Christianity. They serve a valuable purpose. They are, moreover, bound to incorporate propositional statements of some kind. It is true that trust in Jesus and a decision to follow him are the basic necessities for Christian discipleship. The creeds themselves recognize this by the formulation, 'We believe *in* God . . . *in* Jesus Christ . . . *in* the Holy Spirit'. But unless this belief and trust are to be wholly arbitrary and irrational, they must be accompanied by belief *that* certain things are true: God is Father and

Creator, Jesus died and rose again, the Spirit spoke through the prophets, and so on. Hence the classic logical structure of a credal sentence is neither simply 'We believe in . . .' nor 'We believe that . . .', but 'We believe in . . . who . . .'.

The development of the Christian creeds from their beginnings in the New Testament, and the factors which influenced that development are described elsewhere;[1] and there is no need to go into them in detail here. But certain salient features of that development are important.

The creeds are a product of the second great phase of intellectual activity in Christianity, the period that followed the formation of the New Testament itself. It would, therefore, be a great mistake to think of them as a mere stereotyping of answers to crucial questions of faith which had long been decided in the tradition. On the contrary, the age of the creeds was an intensely creative one, when vital decisions on matters of belief were still being hammered out for the first time, and when the whole subsequent character of Christianity could have been changed had those decisions gone a different way. If to some today they seem dry and, in the bad sense, academic, this was certainly not the case when they emerged from the clash of passionately held convictions on matters of life and death, and were greeted on their promulgation with scenes of rapturous enthusiasm.

The wording of the creeds was drawn as far as possible from the language of the Bible. Those who drew them up and ratified them believed that by this means they were safeguarding the true interpretation of Scripture. The formulas were meant to define beyond cavil that essential saving faith on which the varied testimonies of the biblical writers, inspired as they were by the Holy Spirit, converged; and in order to ensure the loyalty of the creeds to that faith the compilers did two things. They selected for inclusion what seemed to them the absolutely essential biblical data; and they made use of biblical words. They did not see themselves as creating some great piece of original doctrinal expression, but as setting out beyond all possibility of misunderstanding the vital elements of the apostolic preaching, so that men might be confident of avoiding error and of laying hold on the truth, and so of saving their immortal souls.

Nevertheless, it was not in practice possible to use only biblical language. Some terminology from contemporary thought was unavoidable, because the problems which forced certain decisions on the Church, and so rendered certain clauses in the creeds necessary, had

1 cf. Appendix B: 'The Origins of the Creeds'.

emerged only in contemporary debate. The content and precise wording of the creeds are at many points dictated by the controversies of the day and by the need to exclude certain prevalent errors. It is more than likely, therefore, that if the work were still to do today, we, in deciding upon a creed, would make a different selection of material; and it is quite certain that in fixing upon the wording we would use our own contemporary terminology and not theirs. We might, for example, include more points about Jesus, or cite different instances of the work of the Holy Spirit in place of the words, 'who spake by the prophets'; and we might well wish to mention the Eucharist alongside Baptism in the section on the Church. Again, so far as language is concerned, phrases such as, 'of one substance with the Father', would never be used today to express any of our beliefs about the person of Jesus, however suitable they may have been in the context of fourth-century philosophy.

One problem, however, and an insoluble one, would be the same for us as for them. As we saw in our earlier discussion of religious language, no human words can ever define or even encompass divine realities. We often talk about the creeds as though the language they use, even if archaic and difficult for us today, was in its own day clear and precise. Nothing could be less true. All such language about God was, and was acknowledged at the time to be, an attempt to express the inexpressible. As St Augustine remarked, when we speak of the Three Persons of the Trinity, it is 'not because the phrases are adequate—they are only an alternative to silence' (*De Trinitate* v.9). Words such as, 'God from God, Light from Light', 'of one substance with the Father', 'came down from heaven', 'and was made man', 'proceeding from the Father and the Son', are helpful to man rather than descriptive of God. They suggest rather than exhaust their topic. Talk about creeds has rarely done justice to this element of mystery, which brings with it a necessary and systematic limitation on the theological assertions we utter.

Valid though they may be, however, we must not let such considerations obscure the fact that the crucial point about the creeds is still, as it was always meant to be, the question of truth. Allowing for all the caveats just entered, the fact remains that we can form some idea of what the creeds intended to affirm when, for example, they asserted the divinity and humanity of Jesus; and we cannot escape the obligation to decide whether we can repeat that assertion in their own language, or whether, while continuing to share their intention, we must express it in different terms, or whether again we have to conclude that what the creeds intended to say is no longer meaningful or not in fact true. Christians do not agree in the decisions they make on issues of substance such as these; and that is why we are all of us bound to examine our attitudes to the contemporary use of the creeds.

What follows is a description of the main types of attitude to this question within the Church of England today. It makes no claim to be detailed, exhaustive, or precise. It is simply an attempt to indicate the range of such attitudes. There may well be many Christians who will not find themselves either exactly or entirely portrayed within any one of the four approaches described but will feel some sympathy for various features of each. To distinguish between Christians solely by their attitudes to the creeds is anyhow unsatisfactory, because the part played by the creeds in the total faith commitment of any individual varies widely in significance from one Christian to another. Such points are in themselves signs of the complexity of the situation, which is such that any one method of analysing it, whether in terms of 'attitudes', 'approaches', 'groups', or 'strands', is bound to be inadequate. Nevertheless, if the reader will co-operate by not pressing the details of the presentation, he will find, we believe, that the substance does reflect certain realities of Anglican life today accurately and fairly enough to support the argument based upon it.

To many members of the Church of England the creeds are a norm of Christian belief, additional to though dependent upon the Bible. For them the creeds not only constitute vital links with the Church's past but also embody the standing truth of the gospel in the present. These Christians emphasize the givenness of the biblical witness both to God and to the Christ who is its climax, and they joyfully discern in the creeds a faithful echo of this testimony and a true delineation of their incarnate Saviour and Lord. Thus they find the creeds to be mandatory for them because they have found the contents of the creeds to be true and significant; they do not embrace them simply because they are received as mandatory by others. They know that these verbal formulas, like the biblical formulations which they more or less directly reflect, circumscribe mysteries whose depth no man can ever plumb. They see no reason why the same truths should not be expressed in different words, and therefore make no objection of principle to the use of variant thought-forms and frameworks in theology where this brings a clearer grasp of revealed realities or a more effective engagement with current questions. But they could not contemplate any replacing or superseding of the historic creeds as official formularies, for in their view it is precisely by the creeds, viewed as classical crystallizations of biblical faith, that new thought-forms and frameworks, and the assertions which they are used to make, must be measured and tested. The arguments of historical and philosophical scepticism against particular credal affirmations seem to them, after honest and careful appraisal, to have no cogency. They think it important that the Church of England should not in any way modify or retreat from its historic commitment to the creeds nor act in a way which explicitly or by implication would stigmatize as unsatisfactory the position of those who accept the creeds *ex animo* and in their entirety. They do not wish to clamp down on the exploring of experimental theologies which for the moment might seem to have left the creeds behind. But they do maintain that any significant weakening in the corporate acceptance and use of the creeds would impair the Church of England's catholicity; and they hold, therefore, that in Anglicanism the creeds are a norm, and that adherence to them is by Anglican standards essential.

A second approach to Christian belief may be described as on balance traditionalist in its general character; but those who adopt it vary in their detailed reactions to the historic credal formularies. On the negative side they have difficulties about individual clauses in the creeds. Sometimes this problem is resolved by stressing the symbolic character of the words, sometimes by emphasizing their historical context. In other cases it may be a matter of reservation with respect to particular clauses. Recognizing that not everybody can be expected to hold identical views either with one another or with the Church of the past, some may view their inability to accept this or that clause of the creeds as of less importance than their identification with the general faith of the Church, which they find expressed in those creeds. The actual difficulties may arise for any one of a number of reasons, as, for instance, the fact that such a clause as that relating to the Virgin Birth may not represent the belief of some New Testament writers. On the positive side, however, they feel that saying the Nicene Creed, for example, at the Eucharist along with their fellow-Christians is one important way of expressing their faith in God through Christ, and of rejoicing in a unity of God's people which transcends time and finds its deepest earthly expression not so much in any words as in the bond of the eucharistic action given by that God to whom the words refer.

Thirdly, there is a broad category of Christians whose convictions lead them to approach the creeds in a rather different way. They acknowledge with gratitude that, for those of them at least who were brought up in the Christian community and whose faith in God was fostered and developed there, the creeds have played an important formative part in their lives. But their allegiance now is rather to the continuing Church of God than to any past beliefs and formulations, which they regard as inevitably relative to the culture of the age which produced them. Hence they can neither affirm nor deny the creeds,[1] because they look to the present rather than to the past to express their faith, and attach most importance to fresh understandings of that continuing Christian enterprise which has its origin in Jesus. They agree that the creeds are *de facto* without rivals as official formulations of Christian belief, but they are in varying degrees unhappy at the thought that they should indefinitely continue to be so. To anyone of this way of thinking the creeds seem to labour under serious disadvantages both as defences of truth and as evidence of concern for truth, involving him, as they do, in solemn and repeated affirmations of beliefs about which he has considerable reservations or which he simply regards as mistaken. Such Christians would, therefore, like to see the Church investigate all possible ways in which it might testify to its profound concern for truth, leaving open the question whether or not these would be likely to take a credal form of any sort.

Finally, there are Christians for whom the essence of their faith is to be found in a life of discipleship rather than in credal affirmation. Such people may have their own doctrinal interpretation of life, but these doctrines seem to them to be relative to their own culture and temperament rather than permanent statements of their faith. They would respect the dogmas of the Church (epitomized in the creeds) as showing, in the language and thought-forms of the age that produced them, balanced authoritative affirmations, excluding false theological solutions and including the necessary theological ingredients. For such Christians, however, both doctrines and dogmas are so inadequate to the living Reality of whom they are the attempted theological formulations that they cannot command full commitment or loyalty. In the best sense of the word they are 'provisional'. Such people do make theological affirmations but they do so by their lives and through their prayers. They commit themselves to the Reality whom men call God as their creator, their saviour, and their sanctifier; and they commit themselves also to a life of Christian discipleship in the sense of loyalty to Jesus and to his values, attitudes, and teaching as depicted in the

1 cf. chap. 2, pp. 7–11 above.

Gospels. They find in him a key to the truth about God and the world, and an authentic way of life. Commitment to God and to Jesus, understood in this sense, is more important to them than 'provisional' assent to credal propositions of any kind.

Christians will, however, be blinding themselves to the realities of the situation if they think it enough merely to recognize the right of each of these types of attitude to exist and to encourage responses of benevolent tolerance between them. To begin with, at least two of these approaches, namely the first and the third, have built into them a powerful drive towards proselytization and polemic. Their views of truth make this logically unavoidable. Those who maintain the first position with any degree of stringency are bound to doubt whether those who identify themselves fully with the third can consistently claim membership of a Church whose historic faith has been grounded in Scripture and firmly based on the creeds. In return, wholehearted adherents of the third approach cannot but feel impelled to challenge the first group equally strongly for an attitude which seems to them irreconcilable with the pursuit of truth in the present. The issues here—on the one hand loyalty to the formulas of the Church and obedience to received truth, on the other adventurous exploration and the Church's engagement with the contemporary world—appear to point in very different directions and to reflect different conceptions of the nature of religious truth. It is, to say the least, very difficult to explain divergences of this fundamental kind merely as complementary aspects of the many-sided wisdom of God. Plainly, when differences go as deep as this, they cannot help generating conflict and giving rise to profoundly felt unhappiness and pain; and the same is true, though not always so intensely, of all such disagreements, as anyone who has engaged in serious discussion of basic beliefs can testify.

It is tempting in the weariness and distress of conflict between followers of a common Lord to opt for a radical and simplistic solution by which a decision is taken to rule out one or more of these competing attitudes. But we are convinced that any such decision would be disastrous to the health of the Church. The tension must be endured. What is important is that everything should be done (and suffered) to make it a creative tension—that is, not a state of non-communication between mutually embattled groups but one of constant dialogue with consequent cross-fertilization of ideas and insights. The quality of this dialogue is determined by three inseparable factors. First, it takes place within the community of faith. It is not simply an intellectual debate but an unceasing effort of brothers in Christ, by every resource of prayer, thought, and common service, to come to the fuller comprehension of the truth they have apprehended by faith. Secondly, this dialogue takes place not only between contemporary attitudes but always in relation to a classical tradition of which the scriptures are the foundation and the creeds are part; and in so far as it is thus related, it feeds on an element which is given. Thirdly, wherever this is genuine dialogue, it is marked by an openness to truth from whatever quarter it may come, whether from other churches, from other religions, or from any authentic human discipline. Thus the Christian pursuit of truth has this dynamic character, that it looks to that which is given, and yet at the same time is ever open to new possibilities of understanding.

There is yet another reason why it is of vital importance to maintain this dialogue as a living reality. Attitudes that are or appear incompatible easily become isolated and polarized, and drift into confrontation and conflict. When groups of Christians have found it necessary to stand alone in defence of the truth they see, the long perspective of history shows that they have also tended, just because of their separation from correctives, to become hardened in error. In a dialogue of faith they can learn from one another's strengths. Moreover, insights and approaches which are opaque in one age become illuminating in another. Even within a single lifetime arguments which at first appeared lacking in cogency may become more compelling. From many points of view, therefore, it is wise to listen, so far as is possible, to the whole range of Christian theological tradition, lest injustice be done to the fullness and balance of Christian truth. The possibilities of mutual influence in dialogue may now be briefly illustrated.

Traditional orthodoxy becomes wooden unless it is constantly questioned. It is all too easy to construe the creeds in a literalistic fashion or as qualifying tests to be signed on the dotted line as a condition of entry into the Church. We need continually to be reminded of the true character of the language they use, and that the mysteries of faith cannot simply be handed down ready-made in a precise formula of words. Our basic loyalty is to God through Christ, not to any exact doctrinal formulation about him; and critics of the creeds are performing a valuable function in so far as they do not let them stand between us and God. So too are the more radical critics who in the name of truth question how far the creeds are right in what they affirm, and who seek to present a gospel purged of what seem to them meaningless or indefensible elements. Theological insights, like moral codes, are always in danger of ossifying as they are handed on from generation to generation. They need to be discovered afresh and re-authenticated, and this will not happen unless they are questioned, charitably but rigorously, and exposed to the acids of scepticism. If they are true, they will survive. If there is anything in them which does not express truth, or express it in an effective way, this may be the means by which the Holy Spirit will guide us into a truth or an expression of truth which we have so far failed to apprehend.

There are, however, also important issues which the traditionalist has to raise with the critics. The creeds echo in a certain proportion and relation the substance of New Testament teaching and preaching. They speak of belief in one God, and of a presence and activity of this God in Jesus Christ, disclosed to men through the Holy Spirit, and of the consequences of this in the formation of the world-wide community of Christ's people, the offer of the forgiveness of sins, and the conquest of death. They point to a gospel which claims to be more than the sum of the insights attained by our contemporary questionings—namely, the gift of a permanent answer to human need. In this way the radical critic's own fundamental assumptions and his elucidation of Christian faith are questioned in their turn, charitably but rigorously; and the whole Christian community can strive to ensure that it correctly identifies what is essential, and does not abandon something of lasting importance for man's salvation.

Bearing in mind, then, what was said earlier about the nature of the creeds, namely that they were carefully worded formulas, selecting and interpreting those biblical data which seemed essential at that time to a definition of the full content of saving faith, how might we see their function in the Church today? In the context of the kind of approach to theology and belief which we have used throughout this report, and of our emphasis on Christian life as an adventure into truth, it is the calling of all Christians to deepen their personal faith and understanding to the utmost by being sensitive and receptive both to the lessons of contemporary knowledge and experience and to the wisdom of the tradition. We have already seen that this has to be done in community, and that it is not a purely intellectual activity. To have the best hope of bearing fruit it needs to go forward within the wholeness of Christian living, which includes prayer, worship, and service, arising from our encounter with God and neighbour and our surrender to the demands of discipleship in mutual love. Such a quest for truth is inevitably, as we remarked at the outset, a lifelong venture; and there can be no guarantee that any of us will come to see everything in the light thrown by traditional orthodoxy, or even feel conscientiously that it would be a good thing if we could. What would be wrong would be a refusal to be open and receptive at all times to the wisdom of the tradition, a wisdom of which the creeds will always form a primary element. But we have to recognize also that Christians are not, indeed cannot hope to be, equally sensitive at all times and in all circumstances to every element in this tradition. It is therefore necessary to have some means of ensuring that those elements which, as we remarked earlier, seem for the moment opaque or unimportant are not abandoned for good but are preserved to make a new contribution to Christian truth and life at a more propitious time. This responsibility can in practice be vested effectively only in the permanent official organs of church life. It is, therefore, their duty to make certain that the creeds, like the scriptures, remain in the bloodstream, so to speak, of the Christian body.

Furthermore, the special significance of the creeds is based not just on what they have been in the past but also on what they are in the present. The creeds are not the exclusive property of any one church. Coming from a time before the divisions between East and West, between Catholic and Protestant, they have in fact maintained themselves, with the Bible, Baptism, and the Eucharist, as one of that very select group of things which the majority of Christians have in common. When churches are growing together as they are today, to jettison or downgrade the creeds unilaterally would be a serious breach of Christian charity and responsibility.

There is, however, no need to shelter behind some pragmatic difficulty in order to be able to give an answer to the question of the contemporary use of the creeds. We are acutely aware that in the particular theological climate of our generation the creeds, by virtue of their unique form as well as of their relative clarity and precision, present many Christians with a sharper challenge in the matter of belief than any other of the classic elements in the tradition. Nevertheless, because, as we have repeatedly said, Christianity as a whole, whatever individual Christians may feel to be possible for them, cannot live without a constant and serious dialogue with its own ever-growing tradition; and because, from within that tradition, the creeds still commend themselves as the most intrinsically authoritative and creative extant summaries of the essentials of Christian faith to a large proportion of Christian people the world over; the right course would seem to be that the creeds should be left in the kind of doctrinal[1] position which in most churches they currently enjoy, but that 'dialogue' should be made a reality by acknowledging that free and responsible debate about their contents and about the best way to use them is not disloyal to the Christian cause.

The creeds themselves stand as a permanent witness that for Christianity indifferentism can never be an adequate attitude, that the many challenges to mind and heart inseparable from the gospel must be answered clearly and forthrightly. They stimulate us to definite answers and to a concern for truth in the answers we give. This is indeed a situation of conflict. But in any community that is truly alive conflict is inevitable and can be creative—and especially creative within a community of Christian charity. This suggests that the true interests of the Church will best be served by continuing to recognize the creeds as the classic formularies of Christendom, and encouraging Christians to discuss them freely and seriously as such. In this way they will continue to be one of the major resources of God's people, inspiring each of us to go on from our individual starting-point and to take no rest, intellectually, spiritually, or morally, in the adventure of our journey into communion with the Love at the heart of all things.

1 Their best liturgical use is, of course, a matter which has in recent years been under review both in the Church of England and elsewhere.

APPENDIX A

The Unity and Pluriformity of the New Testament

by C. F. Evans

There would probably be agreement amongst all Christians that Scripture is normative for Christian belief. Where there is likely to be disagreement is over the sense to be given here to the word 'normative'. In what ways does Scripture rightly operate as a norm, and in particular in relation to credal belief?

If by credal belief is meant a form of believing in which the apprehension of God and of his will, and response to him in trust, worship and action, are intimately connected with and expressed by convictions and statements about his nature and activity, then Scripture (meaning here primarily the New Testament) is certainly normative in the sense that it affords abundant and varied testimony to such belief amongst the first Christians from the beginning. In this Christianity came to be distinctive in comparison with its parent Judaism, which was credal in this sense only to a limited degree, and placed emphasis on 'orthopraxy' or right conduct rather than on orthodoxy or right belief. Jewish monotheistic belief in the one God who is creator of the world and the ruler and judge of Israel and of mankind was always indeed at the basis of Christian faith, and in certain circumstances it had to be affirmed or reaffirmed (cf. Mark 12.29f; Acts 14.15ff; 1 Thess. 1.9; 1 Cor. 8.5f) or stated in equivalent terms (cf. Heb. 11.1,6; Acts 17.22–31; 1 John 1.5; 4.8). It was, however, the conviction that the nature of God and of his purpose for the world had been uniquely manifested in Jesus, his words and works, his death, resurrection and expected return, which evoked credal belief in various forms, so that this God is now apprehended as the one who raised Jesus from the dead (Rom. 4.24), or as the one who had sent him (John 4.34 and *passim*), or as the Father of his Son.

The earliest writings in the New Testament, the Pauline Epistles, are already found employing such statements of credal belief to a remarkable extent in expounding the Christian message and its consequences for human life. Thus, a right relationship with God (righteousness, justification), which is a special concern of the Epistles to the Romans and the Galatians, is said to belong to those who 'believe in him that raised from the dead Jesus our Lord, who was delivered up for our trespasses and raised for our justification' (Rom. 4.24–5). The death of Christ answered by his resurrection is the divine method of dealing with human sin (Rom. 3.24f; 5.10; Gal. 1.4f; 3.13). Along with righteousness the divine wisdom, which is a concern of the letters to the Corinthians, is said to be for believers Christ himself (1 Cor. 1.22f, 30). God's ultimate judgement has been committed to Jesus (Rom. 2.16; 14.9; 2 Cor. 5.10; 1 Thess. 1.10), as also his ultimate salvation (Rom. 5.10; Phil. 3.20f), which salvation will be effected at and through his coming (1 Thess. 2.19; 3.13; 5.23; 1 Cor. 4.5). Further, he stands alongside God as his agent in the creation of the world (1 Cor. 8.6; Col. 1.15f).

These same epistles, however, also afford evidence that such statements had been formulated previously and were already current in the churches. The gospel which Paul carefully rehearses both as to its form and its content in 1 Cor. 15.3–4—that Christ died for our sins in accordance with the scriptures, that he was buried, that he was raised on the third day in accordance with the scriptures—he had himself received from tradition. There are other passages where it may reasonably be supposed that he is quoting an already existing formula (e.g. Rom. 10.9, possibly also Rom. 1.3–4). Scholars have with greater or less certainty isolated on grounds of their rhythmic character what may be called either hymns of credal content or creeds in hymnic form (e.g. Phil. 2.6–11; Col. 1.15–20; 1 Tim. 3.16; 2 Tim. 2.11–13). These may have originated in worship, but they are generally employed by the writer to stress some aspect of Christian belief or life. In the Pastoral Epistles formulations of belief appear to have increased, and are sometimes introduced as such (e.g. 1 Tim. 1.15; 4.9–10; Titus 3.4–8). The acclamations in Rev. 1.5b–7; 4.11; 5.9–10, etc. may owe something to Christian worship. The 'speeches' in Acts, whether they are summaries of what was actually said or are utterances which owe something to what had become traditional by the author's own time, have a common form of statement of the resurrection (and exaltation) by God of the man Jesus to messiahship or to lordship as the basis of an appeal for repentance and faith accompanied by a promise of remission of sins and of the Spirit (Acts 2.14–39; 3.13–26; 5.30–2; 10.36–43; 13.17–41).

At the heart of such statements is the conviction that the purposes of God for the world, and therefore the ultimate issues of human life, are inseparable from Jesus as the one raised and exalted by God to share his rule and activity. Thus belief in Jesus has the same quality as belief in God. It can be expressed in the highly concentrated form of 'to believe into', implying commitment to and ownership by Jesus (Acts 10.43; Rom. 10.14; Gal. 2.16; John *passim*). It proceeds from a recognition of who he is and of his divinely appointed status and function. These may be variously described. In more Jewish contexts the confession might be of him as 'messiah' (Acts 2. 36; 18.5; cf. 1 John 2.22; 5.1), though that term had now to be understood in the light of his rejection by Israel, his suffering and death (Acts 3.18; 26.23). Or it might be the confession of him as 'lord'—the two words 'Jesus Lord' in 1 Cor. 12.3 could be the irreducible minimum of Christian creed. This term may have originated in the acknowledgement of Jesus by the Christian community in its worship as 'our Lord' (cf. 1 Cor. 16.22; 8.5–6), and have been extended as 'the Lord', a title of God in the Old Testament, to express his ownership or control of all men and things (Acts 10.36; Rom. 14.9) by virtue of his conquest of the powers of sin and death and the consequent inauguration of a transformed life (Rom. 5—6; 1 Cor. 6.11), or of his emancipation of men from slavery to demonic powers into the freedom to serve God (Phil. 2.9–11).

Although baptism, which Paul describes as being 'into Christ' and as involving participation in his death to sin with the promise of participation in his risen life (Gal. 3.27; Rom. 6.3–4), is nowhere expressly delineated in the New Testament, nor any credal confession said to be required for it (Acts 8.37 which supplies such is a later addition to the text), some of these credal statements may have been attached to baptism as the means of entry into the Christian community and into the new life (cf. also 1 Pet. 3.18–22). On the evidence of Acts (2.38; 8.16; 10.48; 19.5) baptism was at first 'in (into) the name of Jesus Christ (the Lord Jesus)', and baptism into the threefold name (Matt. 28.19) was presumably a later development. However, in baptismal contexts, as also in connection with credal confession, the Spirit is frequently mentioned as accompaniment or agent (1 Cor. 6.11; 12.3–6; Titus 3.4–6; 1 John 4.2). Although the word 'spirit' is more often used impersonally and is not the subject of credal statement, it is also used personally of one who is distinct and who himself enables the confession of faith (1 Cor. 12.3; 1 John 4.2).

Behind such professions of the faith that emerged after and as a result

of the resurrection, and in some ways preparing for it, stand the Gospels
and the materials of which they are composed. For while the mission of
the earthly Jesus in the Synoptic Gospels is to proclaim the coming
kingdom of God (Mark 1.14–15), the operation of this kingdom is at
times directly associated with the activity of Jesus himself, and the
receiving of the kingdom or entry into it is linked with acknowledgement
of him or attachment to him as a disciple. Some of the Gospel material
would seem to have been preserved in order to attest his status and
function—e.g. as 'Son of God' or 'the Holy One of God' by demons
(Mark 3.11; 5.7), or as 'Son of David' by one to be healed (Mark
10.47f). Moreover, the materials have been so ordered as a whole as to
lead at two crucial points to the profession of his messiahship (Mark
8.27–30; 14 61–2 and parallels). The mysterious and much debated
term 'the Son of man', which apart from Acts 7.56 is found only in the
Gospels and on the lips of Jesus, at least intends to link what Jesus is
saying and doing with the ultimate purposes and authority of God (e.g.
Mark 8.38 and parallels). In the Fourth Gospel much of the later post-
resurrection faith has been read back into the earthly ministry of Jesus,
which is now narrated as an exposition of the continuous and sustained
relationship between the Father and the Son. Here Jesus explicitly
identifies himself, notably in the 'I am' sayings. Further, the evangelist
gives his whole Gospel a markedly credal aspect by stating that his
purpose in writing has been 'that you may believe that Jesus is the
Christ, the Son of God, and that believing you may have life in his name'
(John 20.31; cf. 1 John 5.13).

Thus Scripture is certainly normative in this matter in affording
abundant and varied testimony to credal belief amongst the first
Christians from the beginning. Whether and how it is to act as a norm in
any further sense will depend on what Scripture itself (again here
primarily the New Testament) is understood to be. This understanding
has for some time now been profoundly affected by biblical criticism.
By 'criticism' here is not meant, as is still sometimes supposed, a
superior activity of standing in judgement, whereby errors are detected
in Scripture and some parts of it are pronounced preferable to others.
This may, indeed, happen in the course of criticism, any such
judgements being open to correction by the same methods as has
produced them, but it is not the essence of criticism. This is the analysis
of documents with particular attention to the circumstances that have
given them their character and that account for their being the kind of
documents they are. It is pursued in the belief that in this way individual

writings or groups of writings are allowed more to speak for themselves and not simply by reference to other writings. In the case of the Bible any unity of Scripture as a single whole has now to be arrived at by way of, and in the light of, such individual characteristics of the writings it contains.

One of the chief results of such criticism has been to show that the New Testament writings are frequently the product of a certain development, and embody traditions that have been in movement. Thus, not only is Mark's Gospel established as the first to have been written, but the Gospels of Matthew and Luke are then seen no longer simply as additional accounts alongside Mark's and supplementing it, but as in part adaptations and modifications of it and as written in reaction to it. Even at this late stage of writing the Gospel tradition is shown to be still in movement. Form criticism attempts the more hazardous task of penetrating behind the written traditions to an earlier stage. Without doing violence to them it breaks them down into individual and separate stories and sayings of which they are made up. These separate stories and sayings then appear as having been handed down by word of mouth in the life of this or that Christian community. It then probes for answers to such questions as where a particular story comes to life as being told to meet some religious need, who required to be told it and why, and whether the needs and beliefs of those who told it and of those for whom it was told have affected the telling. Again, particular findings of scholars in this field may be ill-judged, but they are of less importance than the method itself when it attempts to envisage the traditions in these Gospels in relation to particular living situations and contexts. The redaction critic returns by way of the work of form criticism to the Synoptic Gospels as wholes. He seeks to discover what selection an individual evangelist has made of the traditional stories and sayings at his disposal, how he has arranged and organized them to tell a single story, for what purposes and audience he has done this, and whether stories and sayings have been modified for the sake of this whole. He may not be successful in this—witness the number of different accounts that have been produced of the shape, occasion, and intention of Mark's Gospel—but once more it is the method that is important. Meanwhile, John's Gospel continues to pose inescapably the question of what process of development has been at work whereby the tradition of Jesus' deeds and words should attain such a distinctively different form from that in the other Gospels, and for what community or communities and for what purposes it was written in this way. Such types of critical analysis are not confined to the Gospels. For in relation to Acts and the Epistles there is the search for the earliest form of the Christian message, and the attempt to discern its use, application, adaptation, and development in the varied situations which Acts, or the various Epistles, or Revelation themselves reflect. This is a task easier to perform with some of these writings than with others, and with some parts of them than with other parts.

The upshot, then, of criticism in this sense is to bring to light traditions that have been in movement. The movements may have been in the same direction, in parallel directions, or even in divergent directions. Frequently there is not enough evidence to say. If, however, this view of the New Testament writings is not a distortion due to an imposition upon them of a specifically modern idea of development that is foreign to them, but is rather a genuine insight of criticism gained by a method that answers to their character, then it could have important things to say about these writings and about the faith to which they bear witness. It could also have important consequences for their use as a norm of Christian belief. For previously these writings and the statements they contain have been regarded as static in character, as lying alongside one another, all of the same kind and with potentially the same value. They could thus be taken over as they stood, and combined and arranged so as together to furnish the framework of a systematic presentation of Christian doctrine. Such a use, however, becomes less possible to the extent that it does not correspond with the character of these writings as criticism has shown it to be. To give a single example which is not unconnected with credal belief. If the reply of Jesus to the high priest in Luke 22.69: 'From now on the Son of man shall be seated at the right hand of the power of God' is rightly judged to be a correction of the corresponding statement in Mark 14.62: 'You will see the Son of man sitting at the right hand of Power, and coming with the clouds of heaven' which removes from it the thought of an imminent coming (or even if Luke's version is a variant tradition from the oral stage with the same effect), which of these is to be taken as normative, and in what sense of the word 'norm'? Are both in some way normative? Or is what is primarily normative the fact that there has been movement and development in the tradition?

A second consequence of such criticism is closely related. In his book *The Bible in the Modern World* (pp. 91f) Professor James Barr writes as follows of the transition from biblical study to doctrinal statement:

Traditionally, theology was primarily a referential form of study. It sought to understand the entities like God and man, the events like creation and redemption. Its emphasis in using the biblical text was correspondingly referential: its interest lies in that to which the text refers, that of which it speaks. . . . In fact, however, the work of theologians is increasingly dependent on, and concerned with, the search for understanding of the mind of the writers. Only very rarely, as we now realize, can biblical passages be given direct referential interpretation; nearly always they can be used only in conjunction with questions like 'What is the writer trying to do when he says this?' or 'What is the general point of view of the man who wrote these words?' and so on. This is in fact one of the great differences in modern theological practice: even when theology is very definitely based on the Bible, it does not proceed from biblical texts straight to the entities referred to; rather, it proceeds indirectly, and adumbrates its referential interpretations only after consideration of the mind and purpose of the writers.

This change of approach is a consequence of the application of critical historical method to the Bible, with the resultant renewed emphasis on Christianity as an historical religion and its truths as made known through historical events. Many statements in the Bible were made in, and arose out of, particular circumstances, which it is the business of scholarship to reconstruct to the best of its ability. The question then arises how far these statements belong with these circumstances or can live independently of them. The problem of the transition of biblical text to doctrinal statement is how what is intelligible in its original context can be taken over and used apart from that context without in the process altering its meaning.

A third consequence of criticism is closely related, and could also signal a radical change of approach. It is that criticism at least suggests the possibility that there is a plurality of theologies in the New Testament rather than a single theology, *the* theology of the New Testament, which can then be taken over and further explicated and systematized. The advantage of previous attitudes in this matter has been that the instrument (the Bible) was felt to be consonant with that of which it was the instrument (Christian doctrine). Christian doctrine was concerned with the one God and his relation to the world. This relation had come to a head in the one Christ and in the unique revelation of God through him. Oneness was a mark of this not only in itself but also in its apprehension by men, as in the affirmation of Ephesians 4.4–5: 'There is one body and one Spirit, just as you were called to the one hope that belongs to your call, one Lord, one faith, one baptism, one God and Father of us all.' Part of the task of doctrinal exposition was to set forth the unity of Christian truth in all its variety. The Bible matched this in being for all its variety a single entity, and part of the task of biblical interpretation was to show that this is so. In practice this seems to have meant from an early time the adoption of the scheme of things represented by Luke-Acts—the Virgin Birth of Jesus, his ministry in Galilee and journey to Jerusalem, his crucifixion, his resurrection with appearances in Jerusalem, his ascension, Pentecost, and the mission of the Church to the ends of the earth and to the end of time, all in fulfilment of the Old Testament—and into this scheme the rest of the biblical material was fitted. The liturgical tradition reflected this arrangement.

Criticism, however, by inducing the kind of attitude to the text that goes with asking such questions as 'What is the writer trying to do when he says this?' or 'What is the general point of view of the man who wrote these words?' underlines the differences of the various authors in their historical situations. It proceeds by allowing a theology to speak more for itself before it is aligned with other theologies, if indeed this can be done satisfactorily. Again, the question is whether criticism in this way is imposing something arbitrary upon the biblical material and so distorting it, or is bringing to light an essential but previously masked characteristic of it. If it is the latter, then a certain pluralism in theology need not simply be one more surrender to the spirit of the age. It could be a genuine pointer to the character of the Christian message and of the incarnation, at least as these are apprehended by men.

This is not to be exaggerated. There is undoubtedly much common ground and unity of thought in the New Testament. It is often possible to pass naturally backwards and forwards between one writing or class of writings and another. Further, one type of theology may stand in fruitful tension with another, as, for example, that of Matthew's Gospel with that of the Pauline Epistles. It is nevertheless a real question whether the accounts of the work and person of Jesus in the Gospels of Matthew, Mark, Luke, and John can be legitimately added to one another or combined to produce 'the Christ'. It is for this reason that some biblical scholars have felt compelled to use the admittedly infelicitous term 'the Christ event' in order to refer to one who is known indirectly in his effects and through a multiple attestation which may contain antinomies and even contradictions.

A crucial issue here might be eschatology or the doctrine of the end or ultimate issue of all things. This is not only because a recovery of the eschatological background of so much of the thought of the New Testament writings has been in fact a marked feature of biblical criticism, or because in the opinion at least of some scholars a wrestling with eschatology was a major factor in the development of doctrinal thought in the New Testament period itself. It is also because eschatology belongs closely with the idea of oneness, and often governs what is thought and said about the status and function of Jesus, which constitute the core of Christian creed. To speak of God as one in himself and in his relation to men, and of the one Christ and the unique redemption through him, it is necessary to say something, however haltingly, about how God will consummate and bring to completion that which he has initiated in and through Christ. There are, however, very diverse ways of saying this in the New Testament as between, for example, Mark 13, 1 Thessalonians 4, Revelation 21–22, Ephesians 4, and John 14–17. This doctrine perhaps more than any other can be seen to have been in movement. Each of such statements of it can only be fully appreciated in relation to the mind of the individual author, the situation he is addressing, and the rest of what he is saying. They can lie side by side to be thus appreciated for what they are. They can hardly be co-ordinated even in their own terms to produce *the* eschatology of the New Testament, for in some cases one may exclude another, and may even have been intended to do so. Which, if any of them, was still to be regarded as a necessary datum of credal belief would then be a matter of theological discernment, and the criteria for this discernment might not all be provided by Scripture itself as a norm.

APPENDIX B

The Origins of the Creeds

by G. W. H. Lampe

The title, 'The Apostles' Creed', reflects the story that before dispersing to their individual mission fields the Twelve Apostles met and jointly composed a creed to serve as a summary of their future preaching. This story first appears in the latter part of the fourth century,[1] and it is repeated in the first years of the fifth by Rufinus in his commentary on the creed. Rufinus, however, adds an interesting explanation of the need for such a creed.[2] He points out that the word *symbolum* ('creed') means a 'sign' (*signum, indicium*), and he interprets this to mean a sign of recognition. Like Justin in the second century, Rufinus believed that the primitive Church was faced by a vigorous and dangerous Jewish counter-missionary campaign, in which Jewish teachers went about among the Christian communities pretending to be apostles of Christ. The situation thus resembled a civil war, in which the opposing sides dress alike and speak the same language, and in which passwords have to be devised in order to distinguish friend from foe. The Apostles composed their creed to serve as a recognition-signal.

This interpretation of *symbolum* recalls the use in mystery cults of what Firmicus Maternus calls 'special answers' as symbols or signs by which the devotees, like modern Freemasons, recognized one another at their meetings.[3] It is related, too, to the parallel drawn by Tertullian between the Christian's profession of faith and the soldier's oath of loyalty.[4] The common feature is the need for a religious group to acquire an identity of its own and to feel itself to be marked out and differentiated from the rest of society.

The idea that the Apostles composed a creed and that it was the apostolic missionaries who needed to identify themselves by means of it is an anachronism, but there is some truth behind Rufinus' historical

1 *Apostolic Constitutions*, 6.14; Ambrose, *explanatio symboli ad initiandos*.
2 *Comm. in Symb. Apost.* 2.
3 *De errore profanarum religionum* 18.
4 *Mart.* 3; *Cor. Mil.* 11.

fiction. It is true that it was their belief which, in the early days, marked out the Christians from their Jewish neighbours. In Judaism itself the situation was different; its adherents realized their own identity as a community and differentiated themselves from other people chiefly by the observance of the Law. In times of persecution their enemies tried to compel them to eat pork (2 Macc. 6.7; Dan. 3.18) or to take part in heathen worship; they did not usually demand of them a specific renunciation of belief in Yahweh. At the baptism of proselytes commandments of the Law were recited, but the candidates for membership were not submitted to a credal interrogation such as soon became the practice in the Church. The Jew demonstrated his loyalty to Yahweh by his way of life; his religion necessarily involved him in a distinctive culture which was both national and religious and was recognized and acknowledged as such by the Roman Imperial authorities. Even in the cities of the Diaspora he tended to live in a closely-knit and highly distinctive social and cultural group.

A Jew who joined the Church was in a very different position from that of a proselyte of Judaism. For him conversion did not mean that he moved into a radically different cultural and racial group. The Christian way of life, whether or not it included the observance of food laws, looked to the pagan world like Judaism. What differentiated the Christian communities from the Jewish was essentially the fact that they held certain beliefs about Jesus which could find expression in summary, quasi-credal (or 'proto-credal') forms such as 'Jesus is Messiah' (Mark 8.29; John 2.22); 'Jesus is Lord' (Rom. 10.9; Phil. 2.11; Col. 2.6); 'Jesus is the Son of God' (Acts 8.37; John 4.15; cf. Heb. 4.14). Jewish Christians who observed the Law would be distinguished from members of the non-Christian synagogues only by their allegiance to Jesus Christ; non-Christian Jewish prophets and teachers infiltrating into the Christian group would be recognizable not by their life-style as such, but by their attitude to the distinctively Christian beliefs about Jesus. The rejection of the Law by the Christians was in any case secondary to, and consequential upon, their belief about Jesus and their allegiance to him. In the Graeco-Roman world, again, Christians were distinguished from the rest of society less by noticeable oddity of behaviour, as the writer to Diognetus remarked,[1] than by their exclusive allegiance to God and Christ. A Gentile convert to the Church did not necessarily find himself transferred into a new and quite different culture; to a large extent he could continue to live like his neighbours except only for

1 *Diogn.* 5.1–3.

the decisively important differences which were entailed by his exclusive allegiance to the Christian profession of faith in God and in Jesus Christ.

From the beginning, therefore, affirmations of belief (not yet, of course, taking the form of developed creeds) marked off the Christian community from Jewish and Gentile society and gave it its distinct identity. Indeed, so far as the Jewish environment of the primitive Church is concerned, Rufinus' simile of a civil war contains a good deal of truth. Formal summaries of belief were developed in a context of controversy and polemics. They belong to a situation of 'confession' and 'denial' (Matt. 10.32-3; Luke 12.8-9), where the inspired affirmation 'Jesus is Lord' confronts the false prophet's cry, 'Anathema Jesus' (1 Cor. 12.3), where the confessor is assured of direct divine inspiration and the apostate who repudiates the Holy Spirit's aid commits the unforgivable sin (Luke 12.8-12), and where the object of persecutors, whether Jewish or Gentile, is to make Christians renounce their faith (Acts 26.11), curse Christ,[1] or proclaim the Lordship of Caesar in place of that of Jesus.[2] It is in the context of a polemic against polytheism that Paul develops a more extended 'proto-credal' summary; 'For us there is one God, the Father, from whom all being comes, towards whom we move; and there is one Lord, Jesus Christ, through whom all things came to be, and we through him' (1 Cor. 8.6). Another example of an expanded profession of faith, at 1 Timothy 2.5-6, is also related, though less directly, to polemics against apostates and Jewish or heretical opponents, and it is significant that the Pastoral Epistles, which reflect a situation in which Christian faith is on the defensive against strong counter-attacks, are particularly rich in this kind of material from which formal creeds were later developed.

Within the New Testament these affirmations generally take the form either of professions of belief about Jesus alone or of faith in God and Christ. The latter include the Pauline reference to 'us who have faith in the God who raised Jesus our Lord from the dead; for he was delivered to death for our misdeeds, and raised to life to justify us' (Rom. 4.24-5); and this is also an example of the way in which these brief statements were often filled out in order to emphasize certain particular aspects of the Christian gospel. Less often we find in the New Testament adumbrations of the trinitarian pattern of the later creeds, such as the 'Grace' at the end of 2 Corinthians (13.14), the opening address of

1 Pliny *Epp.* 10.96; *Mart. Polyc.* 9.3.
2 *Mart. Polyc.* 8.2.

1 Peter, and the 'baptismal formula' of Matthew 28.19. Similar affirmations occur in Clement of Rome, Ignatius, and other second-century Christian writers. They show a strong tendency to become more complex, professions of belief in God the Father and Jesus Christ, or in the Father, the Son, and the Holy Spirit, often containing extended christological clauses and sometimes also adding references to the Church and the forgiveness of sins, or to other elements in the gospel.

The polemical aspect of 'proto-credal' and credal affirmations persists. Cyril of Jerusalem in the middle of the fourth century tells his class of catechumens whom he is instructing for baptism that religion consists of pious beliefs and good deeds, each as necessary as the other, and that the function of the creed is to establish right belief against the eloquence of the Greeks, the deceitful misuse of Scripture by the Jews, and the poisonous teachings of heretics.[1] To mark off the distinctively Christian position against its opponents was not, however, by any means the only purpose of credal formulas. They were required for catechetical instruction and for the solemn profession of faith made by converts at their baptism. These various uses are interconnected and cannot be assigned to different stages in a chronological order of development. The authors of the late second and early third centuries, particularly Irenaeus and Tertullian, attach great importance to what they respectively call the 'rule of truth' or 'rule of faith' and quote examples of this. This 'norm' is not so stereotyped nor so crisply formulated as a creed, but its contents are parallel to those of the baptismal creeds. It is a short compendium of belief, arranged in the trinitarian pattern, and it bears some resemblance to a modern catechism in so far as it served a didactic purpose. It was especially important, however, as a norm of doctrine and a safeguard against deviations. The Church regarded the Bible, interpreted and understood in the light of the various forms of its own continuing tradition, as the source of its belief and of the pattern of its way of life. The Bible, however, rarely offered a direct answer to the questions asked of it by the later Church; the answers had to be inferred. Further, the Old Testament was already being interpreted in the New not in its obvious or literal sense, but christologically; and the Church continued to read it in its supposed 'spiritual' sense, or typologically. This made it extremely easy for all kinds of conflicting teaching to be read out of the Bible and to claim its authority. The 'rule of faith' was an attempt to distil out of the amorphous, unwieldy, and often bewildering diverse mass of

1 *Catech.* 4.2.

Scripture and tradition a basic compendium of Christian belief which could, in turn, provide a key to the interpretation of Scripture and a norm for regulating its use. Later, as creeds of a declaratory type came to be produced, and formed the staple material for catechetical instruction, creeds themselves served this purpose. They provided a key to the scriptures, a norm for interpretation, and a textbook for instruction. They operated in much the same way as a catechism. According to Augustine the creed is a brief compendium of the truths that lie scattered all over the scriptures,[1] and it provides a summary of what Christians must believe for novices and those who do not yet enjoy a full acquaintance with the Bible itself.[2]

In the earliest full-scale account of Christian baptism Justin says that the officiant names 'the name of the Father and Lord God of the universe' over the person being baptized, and that it is 'in the name of Jesus Christ, who was crucified under Pontius Pilate, and in the name of the Holy Spirit, who announced through the prophets the things concerning Jesus, that the person who is enlightened is washed'.[3] This most probably refers to a threefold interrogation of the candidate in which a trinitarian series of credal affirmations was put to him and to which he gave his assent. Such a procedure seems to be indicated by Tertullian, and is explicitly set out in the early third century by Hippolytus. According to the latter the candidate, standing in the water, is asked 'Do you believe in God the Father almighty?' and replies 'I believe'. He is then baptized once. Next he is asked 'Do you believe in Christ Jesus, the Son of God, who was born by the Holy Spirit from the Virgin Mary, who was crucified under Pontius Pilate and died and rose again on the third day, alive from the dead, and ascended into the heavens, and sat down on the right hand of the Father, and will come to judge the living and the dead?'; and when he says 'I believe', he is again baptized. The third question is 'Do you believe in the Holy Spirit, in the Holy Church and the resurrection of the flesh?', and having again replied 'I believe', he is baptized for the third time.[4]

Here is the *symbolum* (the word is actually used at times to mean the baptismal interrogations)[5] being employed as the means by which a convert identifies himself as a member of the Christian community; and

1 *De Symb. ad Catechumenos* 1.
2 *De Fid. et Symb.* 1.
3 *1 Apol.* 61.
4 *Apostolic Trad* 21.
5 Cyprian, *Ep.* 69.7; Firmilian (Cyprian), *Ep.* 75.11.

since the identity of the Church was constituted by its belief in and about Jesus Christ, it was natural that baptismal creeds should be expanded to include belief about God's work in creation, Christology, redemption, the Holy Spirit, the Church, and eschatological hope. Creeds summarized the Church's understanding of the revelation by which it believed itself to live, and enabled it to draw lines of demarcation between orthodox and heretics as well as between Christians and Jews or pagans. It was therefore essential that all its members should learn and know the baptismal creed, a process which was facilitated as creeds became declaratory instead of interrogatory. According to the regular pattern of initiation in the fourth century, as shown, for example, in Cyril of Jerusalem's *Catecheses*, the creed was taught to the catechumens (*traditio symboli*) during their preparation for baptism and recited by them (*redditio symboli*) after their renunciation of the devil and before they were actually baptized.

Hippolytus shows us an interrogatory form of creed in use at Rome in the early third century. It is in some respects strikingly like, though in others it differs from, the Old Roman Creed in its fixed form as a declaratory creed. The evidence for the latter comes from the fourth century and the beginning of the fifth, but it could have existed as early as the third century. This baptismal creed is attested in its Greek version by the profession of faith submitted by Marcellus, the deposed bishop of Ancyra, to Julius, bishop of Rome, in 340 when Marcellus, in order to vindicate his orthodoxy, presented as his own statement of belief the official creed of the Roman Church. In a Latin text it can be reconstructed from Rufinus' commentary on the creed. It provided the standard form of baptismal creed for the churches in the West, though these exhibited variations from the Roman form, one of the most important of which, the clause relating to the descent into Hades, is first found in the West at Aquileia, the church of Rufinus, having probably come there from the East. By the beginning of the sixth century it is found in an expanded from approximating to our 'Apostles' Creed' in a sermon of Caesarius, bishop of Arles,[1] and by the early eighth century the 'Apostles' Creed' as we know it is recorded by Pirminius (or Priminius), founder of the abbey of Reichenau in south Germany, who, like many medieval writers, supposed that each of the apostles had contributed a clause, beginning with Peter and ending with Thomas.

If the evolution of creeds originated in the peculiar relationship of Christianity to its early religious environment, and developed partly

1 Ps. Augustine, *serm.* 244.

because of the special character of Christian conversion and baptism and partly because of the peculiar use of scriptures in Christianity, it continued and became ever more important because of the tendency to identify saving faith with orthodox belief. Granted that the essence of Christianity was certain beliefs about Jesus, and granted the need to work out their implications for the sake of the Church's self-understanding and the needs of its apologetic against Jews, pagans, and heretics, it is not surprising that this identification came to be made. Thus Augustine could begin his treatise on the creed, *De Fide et Symbolo*, by quoting 'The just lives by faith' and immediately going on to say that the Catholic Faith is made known in the creed. Faith, in the Pauline sense, has been transformed into orthodoxy. To safeguard orthodoxy was the function of 'conciliar' creeds, drawn up as norms and tests for the detection and exclusion of deviationist bishops and other teachers. Creeds of this kind are intended to be documents for theologians. They are, however, based on the baptismal creeds which were meant for all church members, lay and clerical, and the most important of them came in time to be used, in turn, as a baptismal creed.

This was the creed of the Council of Nicaea (325). It was based upon an Eastern baptismal creed, possibly that of the church of Jerusalem. Such creeds seem to have been, at this period, somewhat more diverse and also more fully developed in their theological content than those in use in the West. The transformation of this creed into a normative and exclusive definition of orthodox teaching by the Council of Nicaea, and its subscription by all but a tiny minority of the bishops, had an explicitly defensive object: to condemn and exclude the teaching of Arius. Arius had asserted that the Son, being created, is alien in substance to the Father and is God only in the sense of participating in the Father's deity by grace. The creed therefore affirms the contrary: Jesus Christ is 'the Son of God, begotten from the Father, only-begotten, that is, from the substance of the Father, God from God, light from light, true God from true God, begotten not made, of one substance with the Father'. The purpose and character of this 'conciliar' type of creed is illustrated by the fact that at the end of the Nicene creed the characteristic doctrines of the Arians are anathematized: that 'there was when he was not, and he was not before he was begotten, that he was made out of nothing, that the Son of God is of a different hypostasis or substance, or is created, mutable and liable to change'.

The creed which is today commonly called 'Nicene' (e.g. in the Book of Common Prayer) is not the creed of 325, but is similar to it (though with certain important differences) in the articles referring to the Father and the Son. Whereas, however, the original creed of Nicaea contained no more about belief in the Holy Spirit than the bare assertion 'and (we believe) in the Holy Spirit', the later creed contains an expanded article on the Spirit, reflecting the developed theology of Athanasius and the Cappadocian Fathers. They had argued for the full deity of the Spirit from the evidence of Scripture, the liturgical tradition of the Church (which had accorded equal honour to the three Persons), and the deifying work of the Spirit—for if the Spirit is the lifegiver and sanctifier, and if, as these theologians believed, this cannot be true of a being who possesses life and sanctity only by participation and not by his inherent nature, then the Spirit must be no other than God.

This expanded creed is often known as 'Niceno-Constantinopolitan', for the ecumenical Council of Chalcedon in 451, when endorsing this creed, referred to it as the creed of 'the hundred and fifty Fathers'—that is, the creed of the so-called Second Ecumenical, but actually only Eastern, Council assembled at Constantinople by the Emperor Theodosius I in 381. What connection this creed had with that council is, however, very obscure. The traditional view that the council revised and expanded the Nicene Creed of 325 is scarcely possible to sustain in view of the differences between the two creeds in their christological sections, the silence about the 'Niceno-Constantinopolitan creed' before 451, and the possibility that a creed virtually identical with it may have been in existence before 381. Whatever may be its relation to the council of 381, however, it received ecumenical endorsement in 451, and became not only the norm of 'Nicene' orthodoxy, but also the standard Eastern baptismal creed. In the West it came to be unilaterally modified in the interests of Augustinian trinitarian doctrine by the insertion of the *Filioque* ('and the Son') into the clause concerning the procession of the Holy Spirit from the Father. This controversial addition was first made in Spain at the third Council of Toledo in 589, then in England and France, and finally came to be adopted at Rome early in the eleventh century.

The use of the 'Nicene' and 'Apostles'' creeds in liturgical worship, apart from baptism, began relatively late. Neither baptismal creeds nor the conciliar creeds that proliferated during the trinitarian and christological disputes of the fourth and fifth centuries were intended for recitation at the Eucharist. In the late fifth century, however, the 'Nicene' creed began to be so used in monophysite congregations in Syria. This demonstration of their acceptance of the creed ratified at

Chalcedon could serve to throw into higher relief their rejection of the 'innovating' Christological Definition propounded by that same council. In the sixth century the custom spread to orthodox circles in the East and came to be gradually adopted in the West, beginning with the enactment of the third Council of Toledo in 589, that 'the symbol of the hundred and fifty bishops' should be sung by the congregation 'according to the use of the Eastern churches'.[1] Thus the 'Nicene' creed became a eucharistic hymn, while from the seventh century the 'Apostles'' creed found a place among the prayers in compline, and from the ninth century in mattins and prime as well.

In the Book of Common Prayer the daily offices were reduced to two, Morning and Evening Prayer, in which the principal elements of the pre-Reformation morning and evening offices were combined. In these services the Apostles' Creed was given a central and prominent place. It appeared, not among the prayers but as a distinct act of worship between the last canticle and the beginning of the prayers, and in this position it formed a kind of hinge or transition between that part of the service which was concerned with the praise of God in psalms and canticles and with the reading of Scripture and that part which consisted of prayers and collects. It could be regarded as the climax of the main, scriptural, part of the office, and a further degree of solemnity was added to the recitation of the Creed by the relatively modern custom, based on the baptismal practice of the fourth century, of turning to the east while it was said or sung. Since Mattins and Evensong were intended to be congregational services in which the laity joined the clergy, one result of these changes has been that the Apostles' Creed, as well as the Nicene Creed which the Prayer Book ordered to be said or sung at every celebration of Holy Communion, has played a more prominent part in the regular congregational worship of Anglicans than in that of any other part of the Church.

This prominence has been enhanced by the central place given to the Apostles' Creed in catechisms. Like the Ten Commandments and the Lord's Prayer, the Creed is one of the basic elements in Christian education which the Prayer Book prescribes for the instruction of baptized children in preparation for their confirmation. The catechism enlarged on this requirement. Godfathers and godmothers, the child is taught to say, 'did promise and vow three things in my name. . . . Secondly, that I should believe all the Articles of the Christian Faith.' The catechist replies: 'Rehearse the Articles of thy Belief', and the child

1 Canon 3.

recites the Apostles' Creed, which is then briefly expounded in terms of belief in the Father, the Son, and the Holy Spirit.

The so-called 'Athanasian' Creed is neither a baptismal nor a conciliar creed, and has often been compared with the *Te Deum* as a theological canticle. It was, nevertheless, intended to be a creed, to be used for catechetical teaching and as a norm of orthodoxy. It has nothing to do with Athanasius, being Western and Latin. Its authorship and date have never been conclusively determined, but it was almost certainly written in southern France, and is likely to date from the fifth or early sixth century. Its trinitarian teaching is a succinct expression of Augustinian theology. But although it was not meant to be a hymn, but rather a classical presentation of the belief that orthodoxy is necessary to salvation, it began to be recited at prime from the ninth century, and in the single morning office in the Book of Common Prayer this highly abstract theological statement became, incongruously, a festal alternative to the Apostles' Creed.

INDIVIDUAL ESSAYS
by Members of the Commission

1

J. R. Lucas

The main emphasis of our joint report has been upon the elements of adventure and exploration in Christianity. These are important aspects of the Christian religion, and, for reasons I shall return to later, we need to stress them. But they are only one facet of the faith. Christianity is not only a quest, but an answer. We not only seek the Lord, but believe that we have found him, and that Jesus Christ *is* the way and the life, and also the truth.

Modern man, it is said, finds it difficult to accept the claims of Christianity, partly because they seem to trespass on his intellectual freedom, partly because of sceptical doubts about the reliability or intelligibility of traditional expressions of the faith. Christianity is often thought to be opposed to freedom of thought, and to be essentially authoritarian in nature. Much of the opposition is apparent rather than real. Both 'freedom' and 'authority' are systematically ambiguous, and a man may well be free in one sense while accepting authority in another. There is no law in England requiring belief in the Special Theory of Relativity, but a scientist may still feel that he is not free to reject it in view of the Michelson–Morley experiment. In his science he may reject the authority of the Church or the State, but he relies on the authority of other scientists, and accepts their reports about the observations yielded by their experiments, rather than do all the experiments again for himself. But although scientists rely greatly on authority, it plays an even greater part in Christianity. This is because Christianity is a theistic religion, and claims that the ultimate reality is personal in nature. Persons cannot be known, unless they choose to make themselves known. If the ultimate reality were matter or some mathematical formula or Platonic form, we might hope to discover it by our own unaided exertions. But if we believe in God, we know that we cannot know him, except in so far as he has chosen to reveal himself to us. We have to rely on what God has told us and shown us of himself. We believe that God spake by the prophets and showed himself in his dealings with Israel, but above all in the words and works and death and resurrection of Jesus Christ. These are peculiarly authoritative for us.

To deny this is to deny the central tenet of Christianity, and to refuse to accept any authority at all is implicitly to reject theism altogether. One of the insights that underlies St Augustine's attack on Pelagianism is the sense that Christianity is essentially something which is given us, not something we can get for ourselves. It is only because of certain antecedent actions by God, especially in the life, death, and resurrection of Jesus Christ, that we can know that God loves us and respond by putting our trust in him and loving him in return. Although the Christian religion is something that each man must discover for himself and make his own by a free-flowing choice, it is essentially God-given, not man-made. In the moral sphere this shows itself in our Christian obedience not always coming naturally to us. Some of Christ's sayings were hard sayings; although the Bible, and especially the New Testament, ought not to be regarded as a code of law or as claiming a quasi-legal authority, yet when, as sometimes happens, we find some injunction of our Lord's opaque to us, we may obey it for no other reason than that he told us to, as sometimes we do things our friends tell us for no other reason than they told us to, and we are their friends and loyal to them. It is loyalty, not legality, that leads us to prefer not our will but his. Even so, there is still a sense of authoirty being something other than our own will, which although accepted by us, does lay on us a duty of doing things different from those we would have done had it been left to our free unfettered choice. Although Christ's yoke is easy, it is a yoke, and may sometimes turn out to be a cross. Equally in the intellectual sphere, the Christian is not just following out his own thoughts, wheresoever they may happen to lead him. As a Christian he is committed to the search for the truth, and also believes that the key to the understanding of the universe is to be found in the work and teachings of Jesus Christ. There is, therefore, an essential element of givenness and historicity in the Christian faith, and loyalty to our Lord in our doing needs to be matched by a fidelity to fact in our thinking.

The fact that Christianity is necessarily an historical religion colours our attitude both to the Bible and to the creeds. It means first that Christianity is always and necessarily open to attack on historical grounds. It is part of the logic of Christianity's being a revealed historical religion that the Christian should always be vulnerable, intellectually as well as emotionally, and would have to admit that his faith had been in vain, were certain historical facts not as he had taken them to be. If it were shown that Jesus was merely a misguided zealot, or that he was never crucified, or that once dead he stayed dead, then,

however great its influence or inspiring its message, Christianity would
be proved false, and no man could continue to recite the creeds with
integrity. But it has not been shown, and there are deep reasons, based
on the nature of history and historical argument, why it cannot be
shown. For while it is part of the logic of historical statements that they
could, as matter of *logical* possibility, be false, it is a necessary
condition of our being able to know history that the bulk of our
historical beliefs cannot be altogether false. A person who maintains
that the Battle of Hastings was fought in 1065 or that Queen Victoria
did not exist, is not contradicting himself, and therefore cannot be ruled
out of court on grounds of logic, but can be safely ignored, none the less,
as a self-exposed simpleton. So, too, a man may make out that the New
Testament was a fourth-century fabrication without being proved
wrong by appeal to the principles of logic alone; and this to the
philosopher is an important point, showing one difference between
history and mathematics. But from the fact that historical knowledge is
different from mathematical knowledge, it does not follow that
historical knowledge is impossible, but rather that if we are to attain any
historical knowledge, we must be guided not simply by the single crude
canon of logical possibility but many other, more subtle considerations
as well; in particular, we should be sceptical, not of all historical
authorities as such, but of the know-nothing attitude which dismisses
them all as equally untrustworthy without considering what each has to
say and the circumstances in which each was originally composed. It is
easy to be confused about the different ways in which historical
statements are and are not open to correction. Many theologians in the
face of the logical possibility of historical statements in the Bible being
false have taken refuge in existentialism in order to neutralize this
logical possibility by making it logically irrelevant to their beliefs; but
that is to deny the essential significance of Christ. A unitarian could be
an existentialist, but a Christian takes his stand on the revelation of God
in Jesus Christ. Other theologians take refuge in a dogmatic refusal even
to consider the arguments of the biblical critics on the ground that it is
unwarranted to treat historical authorities with cavalier disbelief. But
that is to misconstrue the role of the Bible in Christian belief, and to
ascribe to the written word an authority which belongs to the living God
alone.

The Bible gives us the basis of Christian belief. We claim that,
however open to critical amendment and reassessment on points of
detail, the Bible, and especially the New Testament, is substantially

reliable. In part it is analogous to what an ancient historian would claim for his authorities—Thucydides, Cicero, or Procopius. The biblical texts have been subject to searching scrutiny. Their accuracy and general reliability have often been impugned. Many Christians have found it unsettling. Nevertheless, biblical criticism has been of great benefit to the Church. It has shown that in general the New Testament is at least as reliable from an historical point of view as any other documents that have survived from antiquity, and has undermined many arguments that used to be canvassed for unbelief. We owe much to the biblical scholars' ministry of devoted doubt. It is only by reason of earnest endeavours to disbelieve the biblical evidence that we have come to feel the full compelling force of its witness.

Two further considerations underlie the special status of the Bible as the basis of Christian belief: the fact that there are almost no other historical sources for the activities of Jesus, and the fact that the Canon was, so to speak, the reading-list of the early Church. These two factors combine to confer on the Bible both a *de facto* and a *de jure* pre-eminence which have a pervasive influence on the sort of conclusions which biblical scholarship could conceivably yield.

Let us conduct a thought experiment. Although the Bible is, as a matter of fact, our major primary source, there are some other sources. Tacitus mentions the crucifixion, Suetonius talks of a certain Chrestus, and Pliny wrote a letter about Christians. The very early Fathers could well have had access to traditions independent of the canonical writings. Even the apocryphal gospels may be searched with some hope of gleaning something true about our Lord not elsewhere recorded. Suppose now a new fragment of Suetonius turned up with a lot more about Chrestus; could we then say we knew more about Christ? It would depend on what was said about Chrestus. In order to identify Chrestus with Christ, enough things said about Chrestus must conform with what we, on the strength of holy Scripture, believe about Christ, for the identification to be plausible. It is the Christ of the New Testament that is the touchstone for the attribution of extra-canonical sources to him. In the extreme, Suetonian, case it is on the basis of Scripture that we determine whether we have secured any identity of reference at all: in the case of the apocryphal gospels it is a question not so much of reference as of truth-value. If an apocryphal anecdote makes out Jesus just to be a standard miracle worker we discount it, because this is not the sort of Jesus the New Testament portrays. If, on the other hand, it seems in character with what we know of our Lord from the New

Testament, then we suspend disbelief; and we are prepared to be convinced by sufficiently subtle New Testament scholars that here we have preserved for us some genuine deed or word of Jesus. Let us envisage further possibilities—a lost book of Tacitus with a full gubernatorial report by Pilate to Tiberius; or we might, conceivably, come across a source—shall we call it Q—preserved somewhere in the sands of Sinai, that both was sufficiently in line with the New Testament writings to assure us of its authenticity and general reliability, and yet would lead us to reject some part of the New Testament witness hitherto accepted. But, equally clearly, there are limits to this process. Although the incidents in our Lord's life are highly corrigible in detail, they cannot be much amended in outline, or he would not have been the Lord of the early Church. Always and necessarily, an account of a Joshua-bar-Miriam who did not go about doing good, did not call the people of God to repent, did not tell them the good news, did not incur a horrible death at the hands of the Jewish and Roman authorities, and did not rise again, would either be about some other charismatic Joshua who excited attention in first-century Palestine or be discounted as a late source or as one stemming from anti-Christian or heretical sources. The Bible is the touchstone. Not only is it our major source, but it was evolved and endorsed by the early Church which was peculiarly concerned with the things concerning Jesus and was chronologically closer to him than we are, and in a better position to reach, under the guidance of the Holy Spirit, a right judgement about certain matters of fact. We therefore cannot improve on it or dispense with it. We may analyse it, argue with it, extract new conclusions from it, but cannot ignore it or sit loose to it or reshape it to fit our own fancies, except at the cost of giving up our knowledge of God made known to man in Jesus Christ.

Biblical criticism has, in fact, increased our knowledge. Not only have critical probings vindicated its substantial reliability, but they have thrown its detailed contours into high relief. Because we can see the biblical authors as distinct individuals, addressing themselves to different readers, with different purposes in mind, we have a truer understanding of the original sense of their writings. The more we realize the differences between what the evangelists were each trying to do, the more our gaze can penetrate through the actual words they used and give us a three-dimensional view of the Son of God. We can reckon with the possibility that St Paul may have been mistaken, or may have been constrained to argue too much after the manner of the rabbis, but can for that very reason obtain a deeper understanding of what he was trying to say, and are then in a position to see that, despite all his human imperfections, he and St John were more than any other men seized with the mind of Christ, and better able to convey to us the fullness of the meaning of what he said and did.

The work of the biblical scholar is thus more rewarding and more difficult than that of the ordinary historian. He needs to be a theologian to understand St John, in much the same way as a man needs to be something of a philosopher to engage in scholarly work on Plato; and just as sometimes a Plato scholar will be guided, in reaching some historical judgement, by philosophical considerations of the logical development of Plato's thought, so the New Testament scholar has to take into consideration many sorts of abstract and general consideration in trying to decide what actually happened, and he may be faulted not on some point of detailed scholarship but on some background assumption which he has taken too readily for granted. It is not a one-way process whereby the biblical scholar produces hard historical facts which other Christians make use of as best they may, but a two-way process in which historical conclusions both bear upon and are based upon a wide variety of background assumptions. It follows that we ought not to take everything the critics say as gospel truth. Scholars are no less fallible than the New Testament writers, and some of their criticisms, for example of the Virgin Birth, seem philosophically naïve. It may well be true that St Luke and St Matthew attached great importance to the Virgin Birth because it constituted in their eyes a significant indication of Jesus' divine authorization, and that this was the theological truth they were seeking to convey. But it does not at all follow from something's being theologically true that therefore the question of its historical truth does not arise. It may be that modern man finds it easy to believe that Jesus was the Son of God even though he also had a human father, and it may be that modern man finds it difficult to believe anyone could be born of a virgin. Neither of these considerations, however, is sufficient for impugning the veracity of Matthew or Luke, or for calling in question the faith as formulated in the creeds.

The argument about the creeds is different, and concerns not the knowability of historical truth, but the nature of the Church, and the needs of the individual within it, and the ways whereby corporate commitment to saving belief may be expressed, and the individual guided in his own pilgrimage towards the knowledge of God. The corporate existence of the Church, like that of any community, depends on its members sharing certain values and beliefs, which must, in the case of the Church, include statements of historical fact. If I believed that Jesus of Nazareth never existed, or that he was just an ordinary man of no great interest to us, or that he was not crucified or never rose from the dead, or if I were to turn my back on him, and decide that the Analects or the Qur'an or the New Statesman were equally good sources of understanding about the nature of man and his place in the universe, then, although I might be an excellent man in other respects, I should have no business to pass myself off as a Christian believer or a full professing member of the Church. Of course, I am free to do any of these things, in the sense that there is no law against my holding unorthodox opinions or seeking solace from Confucius or Mohammed. But I cannot do so, and still be accounted a Christian; I am not free, *as a Christian*, to do so.

The creeds in particular are sometimes felt to fetter freedom, and it is suggested that the Church should either abandon them altogether or replace them with an up-to-date version of the essentials of Christian belief. But it is inherent in the nature of any community that there may be a conflict between the views held by some individuals and those espoused corporately by the community as a whole. The Labour Party has its 'theological' debates over Clause Four, and many communists suffered agonies of conscience after the Party backed the Russian invasions of Hungary or Czechoslovakia. Nor would it help if the Church were to replace the creeds by some simpler profession which stated what exactly the minimum is without which a person really does cease to be in contact with any faith that could reasonably be called Christian. In the first place a large part of the difficulty resides in the fact that religious language is not, and cannot be, exact. Whatever limits were laid down, doubts and questions would arise about whether a particular position lay just within or just outside the permitted range. And whereas in some human disciplines, like jurisprudence, such questions are entirely proper, they are alien to the spirit of Christian theology. Moreover, any search for a minimum formulation of the Christian faith is bound to be uncharacteristically minimizing: the characteristic feature of the Christian faith is not how little it demands of a man, but how much; and this is as true of his thinking as of his doing and his feeling.

It is also argued that we ought to abandon the use of the creeds in church services because the creeds were formulated in different terms from those we should use now, and can no longer be accepted by those who are sensitive to the findings of New Testament scholarship. But these arguments claim more than they are able to establish. It is true that the word translated as substance in the Nicene Creed meant something quite different from what the word means to twentieth-century English ears, and the Church needs to make it clear that it is not requiring the faithful to affirm at each Eucharist a surprising statement of theological chemistry. It is true also that the early Church took it for granted that Hell was a place located below the surface of the earth where the departed spirits went, and that the clause 'He descended into Hell' was inserted not in order to maintain the existence of those infernal regions, but to express the truth that Christ was fully human and in his Passion suffered to the very uttermost, and that his salvation was not only for those who were then not yet dead, but for all men, BC as well as AD. We often feel awkward about the resurrection of the body, because we unwittingly assume that the word 'body' must be used in the sense in which it displaces water in the bath, and not in the sense in which it is conjoined with the pronouns 'some', 'any', and 'every'; and in this case too we need to be reminded again and again of the differences between our ways of thought and those of the early Church. All men's thoughts are influenced by their age and environment, and historians in writing of another age often reveal more the assumptions of their own. Gibbon tells us a lot about the eighteenth century, and if any man in time to come reads the works of twentieth-century patristic and biblical criticism, he will find them a valuable source for the assumptions and preconceptions of academics in our own generation. But it would be wrong to dismiss twentieth-century scholarship on these grounds alone, and by the same token it would be wrong to reject the affirmations of the early Church out of hand. Although there is a gap between one generation and another and between one *milieu* and another, it is not an unbridgeable gulf, across which communication is impossible. I live in a very different world from Pythagoras, but I can understand well enough what his theorem asserts, and that it is true. Although some concepts of New Testament thought, such as sacrifice, are remote from me, I can enter into them enough to have a fair idea of what the original authors meant, and to learn something from them. No doubt, if I were a mathematician, I should not do mathematics after the manner of Pythagoras or Euclid, and if I were a prophet, I should not prophesy after the manner of Amos or Isaiah. But this is no reason for not endorsing what they said; and the fact that if I were writing a profession of faith, I should select different topics and use different terms is no reason at all for abandoning the traditional formulations of the faith. On the contrary, in so far as we are seriously concerned about the dependence of thought upon its cultural context, we should be the readier to believe that any difficulties we have in accepting what has been accepted down the ages may be due to the deficiencies of our culture, not that of other ages. The climate of opinion in our own age is one very subject to fashions and fads. It is a useful corrective to accustom our minds to truths clothed in unfashionable garb, and to take upon our own lips expressions of faith whose value is attested by the whole Church, in many different ages and set in a wide variety of cultural scenes.

The radicals' rejection of the authority of the Bible and the creeds is wrong. It runs counter both to the special tenets of Christianity and to the general character of theism. Nevertheless, it reflects a concern which is peculiarly Christian. Christianity differs from Judaism and Islam in that God reveals himself not primarily in a code or a message but, as we believe, in a person, and Christians see salvation not as being achieved by bare obedience to the word of God, but by being incorporated in Christ and embodying the mind of Christ in our own lives. This entirely alters the aspect of authority in Christian discipleship. Authority, for the Christian, is fundamentally self-chosen and freely accepted. Although there is an element of givenness in Christian doctrine as well as Christian morality, the point of authority is not that it should be simply accepted from outside and obeyed, but rather that we should appropriate it and make it our own. But we are continually forgetting this. There is a constant tendency to ossification in Christianity, both in its institutions and in its formularies; each man needs to discover Christianity for himself, but the words and ways of worship we use often prove earthen vessels which obscure the light rather than reveal it, and convey to others an impression of cold legalism not a living spirit. Hence the many movements of renewal and reformation in the history of the Church, each in turn needing ultimately itself to be reformed. Hence also the fact, embarrassing to Christians, that often our Lord's strictures on the Judaism of his time seem peculiarly applicable to his own professed followers in our time. We too easily convert the New Covenant into the Old. Because we rightly realize that salvation is God-given, we wrongly make our response one of simple obedience rather than a sharing of love, and construe the basic authority of Christianity as based on law rather than on the loyalty of love. The authority of the creeds likewise then appears legalistic and external; and however right it is to maintain that there are truths about God which we ought to believe, if we set too rigid an insistence on doctrinal orthodoxy, we may be guilty of worshipping creeds rather than Christ, and of understanding God as a god who would reveal himself on Sinai, but not in the life and suffering of his son Jesus.

In time past the Church has not been sufficiently sensitive to the doubts and difficulties of individuals, or their need to discover their faith for themselves. Individuals vary. Although many are happy to affirm the creeds as part of their Christian heritage, some will come only slowly to being able to make them their own, and the Christian Church, which attaches peculiar importance to the integrity of its individual members, ought to be particularly understanding towards them. But a corporate body has a collective responsibility which is not reducible to the interests of its individual members. The Church is the body of Christ, and is charged with the duty of proclaiming the good news to the world, and would be failing in its duty if it did not make a collective affirmation of its faith. From a position of firm corporate commitment it is possible to take account of individual difficulties, which otherwise would be, and would be construed as, indications of weakness. In our teaching and our public worship we need to affirm the faith, as we have done down the ages, believing that what we say is true, and will in the fullness of time be seen to be true by those who ponder on the significance of our Lord's teaching and life. But although we must be always telling the truth, we must beware of thrusting it down other people's throats, or we destroy its peculiarly Christian character. Although it is something which is given us, it is not something that others have to take from us, but rather is only real if they can make it their own.

2

D. E. Nineham

It is often said that Christianity is an historical religion. What is meant is that the Christian faith and the Christian relationship to God originated from certain specific events and certain human lives which deserve to be described as historical in the fullest sense of the word. The events and lives in question, although in many cases there was little or nothing to distinguish them outwardly from other lives or events, can be recognized by those who have the key to the realities of the situation as having been acts of God in a peculiar sense. They were the direct results of his initiative, the means by which he intervened to set right the relation between his creation and himself and to make possible the most intimate communion with him.

A homely parallel to the sort of thing envisaged can easily be provided from everyday life. A particular piece of building work may outwardly look, and be, just like any of the thousands of others going on all over the country; but anyone in the know may be aware that this particular operation is due to the initiative of some wealthy philanthropist who has decided to build a hospital dedicated to the treatment of some particularly stubborn disease. The whole thing is his 'doing', as we say. It was his idea and he is paying for it. It is the means by which he is exerting himself to deal with the desperate plight of those suffering from the disease, and incidentally revealing himself as not only a wealthy man but a man of compassion and good will. The parallel of course is only very imperfect, but it may give some idea of what is meant by claiming that an outwardly ordinary occurrence is, when seen from the inside, an act of someone who is concerned to save people, and reveals his own character in the process.

On such a view of Christianity, the Bible is the primary witness to the events in question. It recounts their occurrence and discloses their special relationship to the power and purpose of God. Creeds and similar formularies are then seen as recapitulations of certain aspects of the biblical witness in summary form; and the function of doctrinal theology is to establish the reality of the events, to make clear as far as possible how they produced the supernatural results they did, and to expound, in as much detail as may be, the response appropriate to them both by way of faith and practice.

Such an understanding of Christianity can legitimately lay claim to a long pedigree. According to a recent writer it was Irenaeus in the second century who

> was the first to define sharply the line that divided Christianity from other religions which also claimed the name; the bedrock of Christian belief was faith in a historical person and a history of God's acts. This was the . . . subject matter about which we may speculate, which we may try to understand in multifarious ways, but which we may not alter.[1]

And many modern theologians hold that, although modern discoveries may have necessitated some modifications in the claims we make about the occurrence and meaning of some of the biblical events, this is still broadly the best way in which to understand and talk about Christianity.

Others, however, believe that a more radical reappraisal is called for, and the purpose of the present essay is to explain why they have come to this conclusion. The crux of the matter lies in the extent to which the outlooks and attitudes of human beings—at any rate in the West—have changed in the period between biblical times and our own; but it will be best to spell out some of the issues one by one.

1.   There is first the occurrence of the biblical events themselves: did they occur, and if so in a form which makes the biblical understanding of them plausible? Posed in that form, the question is obviously too general and needs to be broken down into a series of separate questions about individual events. Nevertheless, there is an important general issue involved here, one which is too seldom stated explicitly. Until the emergence of modern methods of historical study in relatively recent times,[2] men's attitude to accounts of the past was generally what may be described as 'authority-accepting'. If a book or an ancient tradition asserted that certain events had occurred, that was taken as good enough authority for supposing that they had, unless evidence to the

---

1 This succinct summary comes from R. A. Markus, *Christianity in the Roman World*, pp. 60–1, who has in mind especially *Contra haer.* i.10.3.

2 It is generally agreed that modern historical study, in the sense in which we have all been accustomed to it since our schooldays, does not go back much, if at all, before the beginning of the last century.

contrary was positively staring people in the face. Little or no attempt was made to question or cross-examine traditional sources. To say that is not to accuse earlier generations of culpable credulity; the accurate evidence and historical techniques necessary for careful criticism were not available, and so there was no general disposition to expect such criticism. The fact remains, however, that, as C. S. Lewis said of people in the Middle Ages, 'they were indeed very credulous of books. They found it hard to believe that anything an old *auctour* had said was simply untrue.'[1] If that applied to *any* old book or tradition, it will obviously have applied with much greater force to the accounts found in the holy Scriptures. So up till the nineteenth century it was true, as Canon Charles Smyth writes, that

> the documents contained within the Sacred Volume were accepted at their face value, and used as data from which inferences could be deduced . . . broadly speaking, people believed everything they read in the Bible in the same way that some people believe everything that they read in the newspaper.[2]

It was on the basis of such an attitude to the Bible that the body of traditional Christian doctrine was built up.[3]

At the time such an attitude was fully compatible with integrity; it is so no longer. We now have evidence and techniques which enable us to reconstruct large tracts of the past (including the periods covered by the Bible) with considerable accuracy—often with greater accuracy than contemporary writers could achieve—and historians rightly feel that professional integrity obliges them to exploit these resources to the full. The modern historian's approach to the past is essentially critical and analytical. Just as a court of law will not accept the evidence of any witness, however eminent, at its face value, but insists on calling as many witnesses as possible, correlating and cross-examining their evidence and then arriving at its own verdict on its own assessment of the whole range of the evidence, so the historian cannot with integrity commit himself to the account of the past given in any single source or tradition, however venerable. He must marshal all the relevant evidence he can discover, written or archaeological, cross-relate and cross-examine it and so arrive at his own independent reconstruction of the

1 *The Discarded Image*, p. 11. Lewis in fact writes in the present tense.
2 *Church and Parish*, p. 159.
3 The same is true of the body of liturgical practice, but that lies outside the scope of this essay.

past. If for any reason this is impossible, for example because only a single independent source for a particular period has survived, he will not be able to pronounce with any confidence on the events in question or pass a verdict either positive or negative on their historicity.

The emergence of this new situation cannot be ignored, though at the same time its significance must not be misunderstood. What it does mean so far as doctrinal theology is concerned, is that a religion whose traditional theology has been based on a particular attitude to the past is now faced with—and in the West is part of—a culture which cannot accept that attitude and must adopt an alternative approach to the past. This is a general truth, involving wide implications, which most doctrinal theologians have not so far formulated or faced up to explicitly enough. On the other hand, it is *not* true that when modern methods of historical study are applied to the Bible it immediately dissolves into a tissue of legend and myth. On the contrary, it would be agreed by all competent experts that the Bible affords a great deal of accurate and invaluable evidence for any historian attempting to reconstruct the periods with which it deals.

Problems do begin to arise for the doctrinal theologian, however, when he comes to relatively detailed historical questions such as are often of great importance for his concerns. This may be illustrated by the vitally important example of the life and activity of Jesus. Practically no serious scholar doubts[1] that in the first half-century of our era a figure called Joshua—or in the Greek, Jesus—travelled round in Palestine carrying out an activity of exorcizing and of counselling, teaching and preaching, often in parables, that he fell foul of the Jewish authorities and was eventually crucified by the Romans. Few would deny either that the Gospels often contain faithful reports of his various activities; but as soon as we ask *which* Gospel reports can be trusted in this way we begin to meet considerable diversity of opinion among qualified investigators. This diversity gets more pronounced when we come to such questions—of great importance to the doctrinal theologian—as the following: what titles did Jesus claim for himself and how did he understand them? Did he believe that his career would prove the immediate prelude to the end of the world and if—as seems probable—he did, how did he envisage the connection? Did he predict his own death and resurrection? Did he believe that his death was a necessary condition for the fulfilment of God's plans and, if so, what

---

1 Exception may perhaps be made for G. A. Wells, but hardly for any other contemporary writer in English.

precise results did he expect to flow from it? What exactly happened in the three or four days after his crucifixion? It is often claimed that even after the most rigorous historical scrutiny has been applied to the Gospels, it is plausible to return answers to such questions which are closely in line with those given by the texts themselves. This is perfectly true, but it is equally true that it is plausible to return answers of a very different sort.

By general consent Rudolf Bultmann of Marburg was the leading New Testament scholar of the earlier part of this century and his studies led him to two conclusions:

(a) that the Gospel material does not enable us to reconstruct the career or character of Jesus with any great confidence or in any great detail, and

(b) that what can be gleaned from the Gospels, when rigorously examined, suggests a picture of Jesus in many ways different from the traditional one.

It is vitally important that the truth in this connection should be stated fairly and correctly. The truth is not that 'modern historical methods have demonstrated the untrustworthiness of the Gospel (or, more widely, the biblical) story', or anything of that sort; Bultmann's opponents have as much right to their interpretation of the evidence, provided it is arrived at in a scholarly way, as he has to his. The fact—the plain inescapable fact which has to be accepted—is that there is wide diversity of interpretation; and where scholars of undoubted competence and integrity diverge so widely, no *one* reconstruction of the events can lay exclusive claim to be regarded as historical in the normal modern sense of the word. Anyone who assures the faithful that 'it happened thus and so' must be careful to add that others no less competent than he is would present a significantly different picture. Since there is no reason to think that this situation will change in the foreseeable future, doctrinal theologians, like other Christians, must learn to accustom themselves to it and its implications. For example, since it cannot be the will of God that our salvation should depend on our accepting as definitely established things which are not, and cannot in fact be, clearly established, we must learn to formulate our doctrine in a way which does not presuppose greater assurance about the life and activity of Jesus than it is legitimate to claim. This will certainly mark us off to some extent from our predecessors, who did assume either that the New Testament accounts of Jesus could be accepted as they stood or, in

the case of the "liberals" of the last century, that they could be made
to yield assured conclusions of a fairly extensive kind about Jesus' life
and character. And as we have seen, what applies to the contents of the
Gospels applies equally to the contents of the rest of the Bible.

2. A second group of questions, which is related, may best be
introduced by way of an example. The two statements 'Jesus came
down from the mountain' and 'Jesus came down from heaven' are on all
fours so far as grammatical form is concerned, and traditionally they
have been treated as being on all fours in some other important respects
as well. Of course no serious thinker has supposed that the Son of God
literally travelled downwards from the sky, but both statements have
been taken as reporting something which happened quite objectively
and both have been accepted unquestioningly on the strength of their
biblical attestation. Modern studies in language, however, compel *us* to
distinguish between them. The former could in principle be shown to be
true or false on the basis of historical evidence, supposing the
appropriate evidence were available; the latter could not possibly be
proved or disproved by historical evidence, however much of it were
available. It is in fact an *interpretation* of the historical facts of Jesus'
life, and so are many other statements which at first sight look like
historical claims, for example that Jesus was the Messiah or the Son of
God, that he ascended into heaven and sat down at the right hand of
God, that his death was a ransom for many. It must be added that the
point remains unaffected even if the interpretations in question derive
directly from Jesus himself.

The matter is of particular importance for this reason: modern
thinkers have become aware that the interpretation placed on an event,
and the way people react to it, may vary widely from time to time and
place to place. For example, the physical condition which is interpreted
nowadays as a diabetic coma and treated with an appropriate injection
of sugar or insulin, was interpreted in the seventeenth century as a
disturbance of the humours and treated with blood-letting either by
chirurgery or leeches. In first-century Palestine precisely the same
condition will have been understood as a case of demon-possession and
treated (if it was treated at all) by means of prayer and exorcism. In 500
years' time, if it still occurs, it will no doubt be described and treated in
yet different ways.

The fact is that people of different cultures interpret precisely the
same phenomenon in different ways; this is important in itself and the

reasons for it are equally important. These are primarily two. First, men of different cultures differ in their ranges of knowledge; for example, the knowledge of body-chemistry we possess in the twentieth century makes it simply impossible for us to accept medical diagnosis in terms of the balance of the four humours. Secondly, every act of interpretation rests on certain assumptions, and the things people take for granted differ widely from culture to culture. The point is put like this by T. E. Hulme:

> It is . . . the things which they take for granted that characterise a period. There are in each period certain doctrines, a denial of which is looked on by the men of that period just as we might look on the assertion that two and two make five. It is these abstract things at the centre, these doctrines felt as facts, which are the source of all the other, more material characteristics of a period.[1]

It follows that if two periods differ widely in the doctrines felt by them as facts, their interpretations of almost every phenomenon will differ widely. Nor is this a thing that can be changed at will. Both A. N. Whitehead and R. G. Collingwood, two of the most profound English thinkers of this century, have insisted that these 'absolute presuppositions', as Collingwood called them, go so deep that it is almost impossible for people to recognize their own (as distinct from their predecessors') presuppositions. It is of course true that we are under no obligation to acquiesce in this situation further than we must; on the contrary, we have a duty to be as self-conscious about our presuppositions as possible. Nor have we any obligation to share in a certain set of presuppositions simply because they happen to be held by a majority of our contemporaries. On the other hand, even if we can to some extent bring our absolute presuppositions to consciousness, we are not at liberty to abandon them in relation to certain areas of reality while sticking to them for the rest. That is what 'flat-earthers', for example, try to do; and it also appears to be the position of those Christians who, when a case of epiletic seizure occurs, unhesitatingly send for a doctor and treat it with modern drugs (thereby implicitly reaffirming certain important contemporary western presuppositions) but insist that epilepsy in first-century Palestine was due not to the workings of the 'laws of nature' but to direct demonic intervention.

We have here an inescapable problem of the greatest importance which is not to be lightly disposed of in the way theologians often

1 *Speculations*, p. 51.

attempt to dispose of it with a passing reference to Dean Inge's rather
superficial quip that 'he who marries the spirit of the age will soon find
himself a widower'. That remark refers to the need to avoid being
carried about by every wind of doctrine at the conscious level. What we
are concerned with here is something altogether more profound which
affects people's reactions at every level and in every sphere.

3.   The significance of all this for doctrine can be illustrated if we stay
with our example of the life and activities of Jesus. Whatever exactly the
facts of his life may have been, the early Christians' response to them
included two elements among others. They repeatedly rehearsed the
facts in ways, and with a degree of accuracy, possible in, and
appropriate to, their cultural situation; and they interpreted them in
categories available in that situation. The only categories in practice
available to them were those of Jewish, or in some cases 'Greek',
religion and these they utilized; knowing no others, they took them to be
self-evidently the right ones. In the case of his Jewish followers,
interpreting Jesus in the religious categories familiar to them meant
incorporating his life into the story about God's continuing relationship
with the world which the Hebrews had built up from many sources and
were at about that time canonizing in the form of the Old Testament. To
be sure, the early Christians recognized that if Jesus was the climax
or 'fulfilment' of this story, his career demanded considerable
reinterpretation of it, but the extent of this reinterpretation should not be
exaggerated. Practically all the earliest Christians appear to have come
from Jewish circles which had been expecting that God would shortly
intervene through an intermediary 'anointed' (i.e. appointed) by him to
bring history to an end and usher in an eternal and wholly supernatural
'new age' or 'kingdom of God'. Jesus was understood to be this
intermediary and his earliest followers all expected the end of the world
to supervene within a generation or so of his lifetime.
    That fact alone means that we cannot interpret Jesus exactly in the
way they did. Our range of knowledge prevents us from accepting any
interpretation of the career of Jesus as literally ushering in the end of the
world; and that is only one example of the much wider problem. Our
range of knowledge and the absolute presuppositions integrity compels
us to share are so different from those of the early Christians that we
naturally find ourselves asking: if men of their cultural background and
presuppositions interpreted the facts like that, how should we, with our
quite different cultural background, have interpreted them? We have
already seen that our interpretation of what they described as Jesus'

demon-exorcisms would have been very different from theirs; must we not generalize from that? If someone with a full range of modern knowledge and presuppositions, scientific, historical, medical, psychological, and the rest, could be carried back on some time-machine to first-century Palestine, is it not virtually certain that his interpretation of what he saw and heard would be very different from any of those given by first- and second-century Jews and Greeks?

4.   Before we begin to ask what it might be, however, a possible objection must be anticipated. Our question is unnecessary, it will be said, because under the providence of God, the Church, and especially the Church of the first five or six centuries, has had the truth about Jesus vouchsafed to it in as final and objective a form as is possible in this world. He was the Second Person of the Holy Trinity become man in the mode defined by councils and enshrined in the creeds. Subsequent formularies have clarified the matter further and made clear at least the general terms in which his achievement of his saving work is to be understood.

From the point of view outlined in this essay, however, this objection is baseless. However fully the Christian Fathers may have been guided by God—and there is no intention whatever of denying that they were—their ideas and formulations remain as subject to the cultural laws governing all workings of the human mind as any others. What they did was to accept the accuracy of the biblical accounts in an uncritical way—proper enough in their time but impossible in ours—and then interpret the contents according to the range of knowledge and the cultural categories available to them. Although their categories differed less from the biblical categories than ours do, they differed significantly and, what is more, the expected end of the world had not occurred; hence the rather static philosophical terms in which they speak, as contrasted with the more dynamic, eschatological, Jewish categories of the Bible itself. The conclusion to be drawn is not primarily that they had 'misunderstood' or perverted a 'pure' primitive Christianity, but rather that they were seeking to make sense of it in a cultural situation which differed both from that of the first century and that of the twentieth.

It should now be clear why Leonard Hodgson was right in insisting that the question with which any passage in the Bible must always be approached is: what must the truth be now if men who thought as they did put it like that? It should also be clear that the question is as much called for in relation to the creeds as it is in relation to the Bible. Credal, or doctrinal, fundamentalism is as untenable a position as biblical fundamentalism.

5. How then should doctrinal theologians proceed? Anyone wedded to the understanding of Christian faith and doctrine outlined at the beginning of this essay is likely to reply: by using modern methods to discover the genuine historical truth about the biblical events and then responding to them in the way appropriate in our cultural situation. That was in fact the approach almost universally adopted by scholars when the situation outlined in this paper began to emerge, and it still has many champions today. It would be absurd for anyone to deny all truth to it, and perhaps it is foolhardy even to question whether it is basically the right approach. However, since these essays are intended to be the expressions of individual views, it may be worth while to explain the grounds on which some modern theologians have reservations about it.

The question is essentially an historical one. Can we reconstruct the biblical events and personalities with sufficient confidence to be able to say what an authentically modern response to them would be? Opinions on this matter have varied widely in the two centuries or so since the rise of critical study. At the present time, so far as the life and activity of Jesus are concerned, an influential school of scholars thinks that we know enough about the historical Jesus to be sure that in him we should have encountered one who made few, if any, supernatural claims for himself, but dared to speak in the name of God; one who, by his teaching and example, would have challenged us to a truly authentic way of living in complete openness to the will of God and total reliance on the power of God—a way of living which he had established as a possibility in all circumstances by his own life and death. As an interpretation of the figure of Christ in the New Testament, when due allowance is made for cultural differences, this has much to commend it; but the claim that the *historical* Jesus understood himself and his mission in these terms is much more problematic. Among other things, it involves attributing to him suspiciously modern attitudes and disclaimers; and on grounds of general probability there seems more to be said for the view of such older scholars as Albert Schweitzer that Jesus shared to the full the knowledge-range and absolute presuppositions of his own culture and so would have appeared in considerable measure 'an enigma and a stranger' to observers from our very different times. We simply do not know for certain, and since the same must be said about many other biblical accounts and events, is it not better to adopt an altogether different approach?

6. If there is any truth at all in Christianity, the events behind the biblical accounts, whatever exactly they may have been, must have been intended by God to issue, as they did, in the existence of a new community, the Christian Church, in which men and women of all generations since, including our own, have been able to find forgiveness, reconciliation with God, and release of their energies from the service of self for the service of others. Just as the precise course of the events which gave rise to the community and its communion with God is often beyond our knowing, so is the way God produced the community and its common life from the events. The events formed a whole and their effect was a single whole effect. It looks as if we are not meant or permitted to break the story into parts and attribute the whole effect to one part or to ascribe any particular part of the effect to any particular event in the story. That this succession of events had the result it did—a new community in which are found a new forgiveness, victory, and hope—is something Christians know for a fact; but it is God who made the events significant in this way, and precisely how he did it is beyond our knowing. It is impossible for us to explain, and perhaps presumptuous even to try to explain, just where and how in the whole story God was at work. 'His secret to himself.'

Given their historical situation and their habits of thought, such reverent agnosticism was scarcely possible for the first Christians. They sought to explain, often in mythical terms, the 'mechanics' of the way their new-found peace with God and man had been produced, and to attribute certain elements in their situation to certain events in the story they told. For example, since they now knew themselves to have free access to God and his grace despite the undeniable fact that they were sinners; and since the doctrine that 'without the shedding of blood there is no forgiveness' was one of those felt in their period as a fact; they more or less automatically interpreted Jesus' death as a sacrificial blood-shedding efficacious for the forgiveness of all (or as some of them held, almost all) sin.[1]

---

1 This point has been highly compressed in the interests of brevity. There must have been things about the career and teaching of Jesus which gave rise to the early Christians' conviction of reconciliation with God, and it seems likely that the manner of his death was among them. In historical fact the interweaving of event and interpretation will have been much more complicated and continuous than our

In this general approach later generations have followed them. Taking the biblical events as an unquestioned and unquestionable starting-point, they have sought to explain and understand them in the light of the various world-views and categories of their respective times, often subtly reinterpreting the biblical symbolism and terminology in the process.

It would be easy to be misled by this procedure. It is one of the most important cultural differences between people of many earlier periods and ourselves that their attitude to the past was very different from our own; as late as the eighteenth century, for example, a highly intelligent man such as Bolingbroke could define history as 'philosophy teaching by examples'. In many periods of the past people were quite content to say positively that things had happened thus and so (in a way we should not dare to do without chapter and verse to support our account) when what was really in their minds was: God being what he is, and things being what they are, the past '*must* have been' thus and so for the present to be what it is.[1] Their statements about the past, even when by our standards they appear completely unambiguous, are thus very often evidence principally for their current beliefs. We have quoted one example above: if the early Christians knew themselves forgiven, then the death of Jesus 'must have' provided the necessary atonement. Similarly, if Jesus was a divine figure, then the really significant part in his conception—which according to ancient ideas was the male part—'must have been' played directly by God; Jesus 'cannot have had' any human father.

If we recognize this, we shall approach these writings in a new way as evidence for the faith and experience of which they are—in very various ways—the expressions. And to what end? Perhaps at the risk of gross oversimplification it may be put like this.

7.   Essentially what the Church has done is to make available to men of each generation the possibility of union and communion with God. Usually without being fully conscious of what they were doing, preachers have presented this possibility in different terms at different

oversimplified account suggests. The point is, however, that we cannot now tell exactly which of 'the things concerning Jesus' it was that gave rise to the conviction of reconciliation with God and so we do not know if they would have produced the same conviction in people of our cultural outlook.

1 See the very instructive remarks of the distinguished medievalist Sir Richard Southern in his book, *Western Society and the Church in the Middle Ages*, pp. 92–3.

times in order to make it intelligible and acceptable to people of different cultural backgrounds. It is precisely because, under the providence of God, they have done this that the possibility reached our time in a form intelligible and acceptable with integrity by us. Even in the form in which it was proclaimed a hundred years ago the Christian faith would not be a live option for most people today. As it is, it has made sense to us and we have been gratefully able to accept it. Yet most Christians today find that in the precise form in which they received the tradition—from parents, teachers, or preachers—it will not do. The fit is seldom perfect; the shoe pinches at one or more points. The task of doctrinal theology is to get the fit right for men of our culture; to understand and formulate the faith in a way acceptable with integrity today—which does not of course mean removing the mystery and genuine incomprehensibility by which all attempts to speak of the supernatural are bound to be attended. It means removing all *unnecessary* obstacles to acceptance of the faith, which have arisen simply as a result of cultural change, and relieving us of any necessity to 'believe what we know cannot possibly be true'.

If there is any substance in what has been said in this paper, it will be evident that doctrinal theologians in essaying this task cannot expect to find direct or definitive answers to their twentieth-century questions in the beliefs and formularies of earlier generations, even the biblical generations. Paradoxically, our generation is in some ways closer than the intervening generations have been to the earliest Christians; they had no Christian scriptures, creeds, or traditions to rely on but had to speak 'as the Spirit gave them utterance'. Discovering what the Spirit would now say to the churches, so far as it depends on human effort, will involve sensitive recourse to many different sources not all of them traditional, indeed not all of them religious at all in the restricted sense of the term; it will involve recognition that discovering the Christian gospel for today is a task for the Christians of today and that, as Leonard Hodgson said, it is a mistake to 'assume that someone somewhere, at some time in the past, really knew the truth and that what we have to do is to find out what he thought and get back to it'.

Yet, if a modern creed cannot simply be deduced from any previous Christian formulations, even those of the biblical writers, that is not to deny these formulations a vitally important role. What is the aim of the Christian? It is, as it has always been, so to open himself to God that the spirit of God may penetrate, inform, and shape the whole of his life in every part and at every level. In his effort to learn what that means and how it is brought about, he will gratefully avail himself of all the help that is forthcoming, and one of his chief and indispensable resources will be the records of the faith, discipleship, and relationship to God of his predecessors down the ages. It is in this connection that a lot of what we have been saying becomes relevant. The modern Christian must learn how to read with understanding what his predecessors have written in their various cultures, recognizing that much of it is in effect commentary on earlier writings (the New Testament itself has illuminatingly, if onesidedly, been described as a commentary upon the Old) and that in much of what they have to say about the past they were in fact projecting the faith and experience of their own period on to history in the fashion we have described. If we discover how to read their writings in the appropriate way we may learn to 'think the thoughts of our predecessors after them'. To do so requires a considerable exercise of sympathetic imagination and of what Coleridge called 'willing suspension of disbelief', and it is difficult to specify briefly precisely what sort of help can be expected to be forthcoming. At least this can be said, however, on the basis of personal experience; to 'pass over' into the thought, faith, and experience of earlier Christians is to open up the possibility of returning to the present with one's faith deepened, broadened, and renewed, one's unfaith rebuked, one's fears and frettings stilled, and one's path made clear.[1]

It will nevertheless remain true that the story the modern Christian tells, the images and symbols in which he gives expression to God's dealings with men—and all talk about God is bound to be in the form of image and symbol—will have to be compatible with the rest of his knowledge of reality and appropriate to his cultural situation. It is a large part of the function of doctrinal theology to help to ensure that they are.

1 For further illustration on that see the remarkable recent book by the Roman Catholic writer John S. Dunne, *The Way of All the Earth* (Sheldon Press 1973).

3

C. P. M. Jones

Henry VIII took the Church of England out of Europe; and in the next reign Cranmer started the practice of promulgating national liturgies as appendixes to Acts of Uniformity. Only after Elizabeth I had re-established an all-inclusive national Church did attention turn to matters of doctrine; in 1563 the Thirty-Nine Articles were agreed upon, in almost their present form, and from 1571 the clergy had to subscribe to them, the first and last statement of distinctive Anglican teaching designed to cover all disputed matters and to be accepted by all. But on closer inspection these articles only stake out areas within which Christian teaching may operate; they provide no coherent rationale or theology, beyond their practical, almost political, purpose. Continental Christians of all confessions must have been stupefied by this insular and bizarre combination of virtually unreformed polity, shorn catholic ritual, and modified Calvinist theology, an unstable amalgam held together in a strong Erastian framework. This Anglicanism was certainly a polity in search of a theology; and when the theology begins to appear towards the end of the century, in answer to persistent Puritan attack, Richard Hooker chooses to write on the *Laws of Ecclesiastical Polity*.

From Hooker and his successors of the seventeenth century, Dr McAdoo has distilled *The Spirit of Anglicanism* (1965); he finds no theological system, but 'a specific theological method which, varying its stress according to the demands of different situations, consists in the appeal to Scripture, to antiquity and to reason' (pp. v–vi), 'a threefold cord not easily broken' (p. 80). They appeal to Scripture, not for minute guidance on civil or ecclesiastical discipline, but for infallible assurance of eternal life and all that is necessary to attain it. In the appeal to antiquity and early Christian tradition, there are divergent evidences and conclusions, which nevertheless tend to support the English establishment against Rome and Geneva. The appeal to reason, supremely in Hooker, but also in others, turns out to be heavily dependent on Aquinas's teaching about law, divine and eternal in God, and natural in his diverse creatures, of which all positive law, civil, international, or ecclesiastical, is an application and reflection. Dr McAdoo admits that this happy synthesis is not obtainable in all seasons and in all intellectual climates. He sees it flourishing again in late nineteenth-century Oxford, in Charles Gore and his collaborators in *Lux Mundi*, under the influence of T. H. Green's version of Hegelian idealism, supporting a moderate scriptural criticism, and vivified by a new sense of church tradition and communion. But he can cite no other instance. The aspiration of the Christian mind towards a unified coherence of all truth, natural and supernatural, the acme of the theological quest, can rarely reach its goal in this world; William Temple abandoned his search for 'a Christocentric metaphysic' three years before his death. But we should not be surprised or disappointed; the quest for clarity and coherence is on the same footing as the quest for charity and sanctity, and in neither case will God or our conscience let us rest.

But where can the contemporary Christian begin his *reconstruction of belief*? Naturally we would like to begin with reason. We cannot rule out in advance any attempt at natural or rational theology, moving towards the divine from nature or from men and from our experience of life; but we must recognize that such attempts, in the present climate, are difficult and precarious. For we have no running start; there is no generally accepted philosophy to which we can appeal and on which we can build, as Hooker built on Aquinas and Gore's friends on T. H. Green. And in our appeal to Scripture we are a long way from Hooker, and even from Gore; chapter 4 of this report reveals a very exciting state of affairs in our modern understanding of the sacred writings; all flux, but no rock; invigorating for convinced believers, but perplexing for others. Even the figure of Jesus is difficult to grasp in a climate in which it is widely held that the four Gospels tell us more about the evangelists and their churches than they tell us about him, and that the Acts of the Apostles tell us more about St Luke than about St Peter and St Paul. We are left with tradition; but what tradition? We think first of the Anglican tradition, and not entirely without reason, as tradition in the form of inertia has probably kept us where we are. But Anglican tradition is no more self-authenticating now than it was before Hooker wrote; and it needs more justification still in our present ecumenical context. The Anglican appeal to history and tradition is not an appeal to Anglican history and tradition, except in so far as that tradition contains, preserves, and is enriched by tradition more central, universal, and fundamental than itself; in other words by the catholic tradition of the universal Church, Eastern and Western. And that tradition is as difficult to discover *in detail* as it was in the seventeenth century. And yet it may have a central core, essential Christianity; but if Christianity is, and was, a living thing, 'tradition' is an odd word to use for it. Perhaps we really mean the Christian life as lived in the Christian community; and tradition is only a small part of that. On the other hand, at the heart of the Christian life and the Christian community, as we believe and perhaps experience, is Christ himself; is he the antithesis of tradition, or is he the very substance of it?

Many modern Christians, under the guidance of Vatican II, do not draw a rigid line between 'Scripture' and 'tradition'; 'both flow from the same divine source' (*de Revelatione* II. 9). Is this just pious Roman rhetoric, and can it be related to the realities of modern New Testament study? Or, put another way, are the Gospels, and their authors, the sole source of our knowledge of Christ?

> Since none of the Gospels can have been written down in their present form before the second half of the first century, the Pauline Epistles are the earliest Christian documents which survive. The Epistles, therefore, offer important evidence of the primitive Christian tradition in those passages where St Paul refers to the teaching he had 'received'; and where, when writing to those who had not been converted through his preachings, he assumes certain beliefs to be held by all Christians alike.

These words of Sir Edwyn Hoskyns, though written in 1926,[1] have lost none of their truth and force; rather the opposite, as St Paul's *obiter dicta*, thrown off in the course of his pastoral correspondence, can provide historical information of the highest quality, especially when compared with the more self-conscious stance detectable in the evangelists (at least in St Luke, cf. Luke 1.1–4). Hoskyns refers to two types of evidence; the latter is best instanced in the letter to the Roman church, as yet unvisited, where he can assume that the Roman Christians have been handed over ('traditioned') to a 'definite pattern of teaching' (Rom. 6.17), though the pattern is not specified in the context. The former type of evidence, where St Paul cites received teaching, is to be found chiefly in the first letter to the Corinthians, and pre-eminently in the famous passage at the beginning of the chapter (15) on the resurrection, which we must examine in detail. We must remember that St Paul's relations with his community at Corinth were never easy; at

1 *Essays Catholic and Critical*, p. 162.

Corinth, as in Galatia, there were dissident factions ready to pounce on any inaccuracy or misrepresentation of fact or common teaching, and in particular some kind of 'Cephas party', jealous of teaching connected with the leader of the Twelve.

> For I handed on to you first of all [in time or importance] that which I
>   also received:
> that Christ died for our sins according to the scriptures;
> and that he was buried;
> and that he was raised on the third day, according to the scriptures:
> and that he was seen by Cephas, then the twelve . . .
>   (1 Cor. 15.3–5)

So there was a common form of teaching about these central Christian tenets before his conversion, by receiving which he himself came to share and proclaim the common apostolic message (see v. 11). He sees his own conversion and commission as the fruit of the last of the series of distinct and recordable appearances of the risen Christ (v. 8). He firmly holds that his apostolic commission comes direct from God (Gal. 1.1, 12), but this is not incompatible with receiving teaching about Christ, for which presumably he went to Jerusalem 'to get information from Cephas' (Gal. 1.18). The language of the passage confirms that St Paul is quoting rather than writing freely in his own style; and he uses the technical terms of the rabbis for the *receiving* and *handing on* of authoritative teaching. Moreover, again following rabbinic practice, each clause may be a condensed summary for mnemonic purposes of one aspect of the Gospel tradition, which would be treated in fuller detail in the course of preaching and oral instruction.

When we turn from the form to the content of this authoritative tradition of teaching, we may well be surprised, particularly if we have been brought up to make a clear distinction between fact and interpretation. Here the fact would be 'Jesus died'; that he is named as Christ or Messiah, and that he died 'for our sins', and that all this happened 'according to the scriptures', would be interpretation, a Christian gloss on an event that was either 'neutral' or capable of other interpretations. As Leonard Hodgson used to like to quote from Whitehead, 'The Buddha gave his doctrine to enlighten the world: Christ gave his life. It is for Christians to discern the doctrine';[1] in other words, all doctrines of atonement are Christian additions to, or impositions on, Christ's death. And we find this kind of 'interpretation'

---

1 *For Faith and Freedom* I, p. 111.

in our earliest record of the 'facts'. Let us confine ourselves to the statement about the death. 'According to the scriptures' may refer to particular passages of the Old Testament (such as Isa. 53), or to the Old Testament as a whole. Christ's death can only be understood in the light of the Jewish inheritance: St Paul himself gives many examples of such interpretation, as when he describes Christ in his death as 'our passover lamb' (1 Cor. 5.7) or as 'mercy-seat' (Rom. 3.25), scriptural images somewhat external to the event. 'For our sins', to deal with our sins (Rom. 8.3), can be seen as a special application of this scriptural interpretation to the Lord's death: and both examples of an external, though clearly collective, interpretation. Can we get nearer?

By an extraordinary coincidence in this same letter St Paul has occasion to cite another item of 'tradition' in connection with irregularities in the eucharistic practice of the Corinthian assembly (11.23–5), a tradition he had also faithfully *received* and *handed on*. This is the tradition about the supper on the night of Jesus' betrayal. He says he received it 'from the Lord', a phrase which is more likely to mean that the Lord was the ultimate source of the tradition than that St Paul had learned it by direct revelation. This passage has complications not present in the other, in that it has its equivalent in the (later) Gospel of St Mark (14.22–5), and together with the Marcan account seems to underlie the narrative of St Luke (22.15–20, longer text). Much could be, and has been, written, comparing the Pauline and the Marcan accounts of the Last Supper, notably by Dr Jeremias in the best-known book on the subject, *The Eucharistic Words of Jesus*. There he painfully argues towards the conclusion that in an abbreviated version of the parallel sayings in St Mark (this [is] my body . . . this [is] my blood . . .) we have the authentic words of Jesus over the bread and wine. Nevertheless, we must recognize that the earlier, Pauline, narrative preserves features of the original occasion, absent from St Mark's account, which must be considered seriously in the search for valid historical evidence.

(*a*) The bread and cup are given, not in the course of the meal (Mark 14.22), but on either side of it, separated by it ('after dining, the cup', 1 Cor. 11.25), in line with Jewish custom on festal occasions.

(*b*) The double command to repeat the ordinance, which would be made necessary by that separation on the original occasion, and might prove superfluous later after the rite had become established custom.

(*c*) The absence of commands to eat and drink presupposes normal

Jewish custom; the Marcan commands reflect a ritual act divorced from its original context.

(d) The fact that the eucharistic words of Jesus, as represented in the Pauline tradition, are *not* parallel should be considered in favour of their authenticity; while the parallelism in St Mark may reflect an adjustment through liturgical usage.

(e) Both accounts make use of the covenant image in connection with the cup and the blood, but in different ways, 'This cup is the new covenant in my blood' (Paul); 'This [is] my covenant-blood' (Mark). Mark's version is an adaptation of Moses' declaration in Exodus (24.8) at the inauguration of the covenant, while Paul's is more dependent on the prophecy of Jeremiah (31.31–4) concerning a new internal and effective covenant. Jeremias concludes from this divergence that the covenant reference is not part of the original saying of Jesus; others may infer that a covenant reference of some kind must be original in order to account for the two early variations. Moreover, the covenant references are not incompatible; if Jesus referred to a covenant to be inaugurated in his own blood, both Exodus 24 and Jeremiah 31 are presupposed as the necessary background.

This diversion leads us back to the interpretation of Christ's death 'for our sins according to the scriptures' (1 Cor. 15.3). Certainly in St Paul's understanding, and, as we have tried to show, in all probability in solid historical fact as well, this interpretation was not just a Christian imposition on the Lord's death; it was an extension of, and an entering into, the Lord's own understanding of his death when he took the scriptural type of the covenant between God and Israel, inaugurated in blood, and used it to explain his own blood-shedding for the inauguration of a new and better covenant, in which, as Jeremiah (31.34) had envisaged it, 'I will forgive their iniquity, and their sin I will remember no more'. 'Interpreting in advance the significance of his coming passion, he was in effect making it to be, for all time, what it otherwise would not have been, viz: a sacrifice for the sins of the world.'[1]

In thus trying to establish the earliest official, authoritative, and universal understanding of the gospel of Christ's death and its historical ground in the expressed mind of Jesus, we hope we have demonstrated an important link between the thought of Jesus and that of the nucleus

1 A. E. J. Rawlinson in *Mysterium Christi* (1930), p. 241.

of his followers, and that at a central and nodal point in the understanding of the gospel in which, as St Paul says (1 Cor. 15.3), Christian converts are established and are in the process of salvation. We have also established, outside the four Gospels, a sequence of events which can be regarded as a framework at least for the passion narratives in the Gospels. We also find in this tradition of Christ's death and resurrection the starting-point of much of St Paul's more elaborate and original thinking about the divine ground of salvation in Christ (e.g. Rom. 1.2–4; 4.25; 5.9–11; 1 Cor. 1.29–31; 15.20–2, etc.) as well as about the nature of the Christian life (e.g. Rom. 6.1–11; 2 Cor. 4.10–12; Col. 2.11–15; 3.1–17, etc.).

Perhaps we have here the distinctive core of all Christian theology and life. After an exhaustive catalogue of the various trends, often incompatible, which can be noted in recent theology, *The Fourth R*, the report on religious education of a commission presided over by our late chairman, concludes (para. 109, pp. 55, 56):

> This picture of the contemporary concerns of theology, intricately varied and complex though it is, does not of course deny but rather implies that in the Christian faith there is something 'given', something to be taken as a base, which all these different views variously articulate. At the same time we recognize that in their desire to be creative by abandoning some traditional images, or to open up discussion by pointing to the limitations of any language which seeks to express the mystery and infinitude of God, and in their desire to show integrity in their handling of current biblical scholarship, even Christian writers have sometimes given the impression that Christian language talks about nothing in particular. It is therefore important to recall that the different strands of Christian doctrine and differing Christian moral judgements arise around, are ultimately derived from, and point back to God's activity in Christ, what can be spoken of as 'the grace of the Lord Jesus Christ, the love of God, and the fellowship of the Holy Spirit'. It is to this givenness about the Christian faith which lies behind all its articulation that we must point if we would respond on the one hand to the critic who asserts that the multiple strands of theology talk about nothing, and on the other hand to the teacher who is baffled and even dispirited by the bewilderingly intricate variety which the theological scene presents to him.

The 'tradition' recorded in 1 Cor. 15.3–5 is not a 'dead' tradition of

pharisaic custom or of archaeological detail; it is a 'living' tradition
about the past and present activity of a living person, or rather a dead-
and-alive person, which can result in visible effects, like the conversion
and energizing of St Paul and the dynamic of the apostolic mission. The
words of Pio Nono, *La Tradizione son'Io*, apply better to Jesus Christ
than to himself. But the words of the tradition can become a pharisaic
rigmarole if they are divorced from their place in the apostolic
movement and the divine movement for the salvation of the world
which it embodies; in other words, without the Holy Spirit, in whose
power alone men can confess Jesus as Lord (1 Cor. 12.3), who alone
can impart to us a share in the wisdom of God's plan in Christ (1 Cor.
2.10), and who can make the Lord Jesus a reality for each succeeding
generation (John 16.12–15). The divine and the human activities are not
alternatives or incompatibles; the divine works in and through, and all
round, the human. The apostle is converted to proclaim the message
entrusted to him; he imparts it as well as he can, but it only bears fruit as
God himself is at work in his hearers, enabling them to hear through his
human words the divine invitation to glory (1 Thess. 2.1–13). The living
Spirit does not supplant, or dispense with, the definite gospel and the
authoritative teacher, but works along with them and through them,
while they set out not to be autonomous organs of revelation, but to be
contributory parts of a larger whole.

The tradition of Christ's death and resurrection may be at the centre,
but is not the whole of the redeeming work. St Paul elsewhere describes
his conversion and commission in different language: 'God was pleased
to reveal his son to me' (Gal. 1.16). From this, as from other references
(e.g. Gal. 4.4; Rom. 1.2; 8.3; 8.29), St Paul, to the scandal of all Jewish
and many Christian students of Christian origins, regards the divine
and antecedent sonship of Jesus as a cardinal Christian truth. If he
describes his conversion in this way, it may have provided the secret
clue to his own perennial theological quest, to understand how it was
possible that in God's plan the people of God should crucify the unique
and special Son of their own God; he is led to think of fall, sin, and law;
of the image of God identifying himself with fallen Adam to renew the
race from within. Here again there is a correspondence between St Paul
and the synoptic evangelists; for what he attempts theologically, and
mainly in fits and starts, they, led by St Mark, attempt dramatically
as they show how one designated as Son of God comes to crucifixion
and resurrection. And the theologians of the New Testament, the fourth
evangelist, and the author of Hebrews rationalize and integrate certain

elements of the primitive scheme. In many different degrees and in many different fashions the divine truth is presented to us in either testament, but all are held together by the Son who came to live and die and rise again as man for the salvation of the world. This is the central, co-ordinating truth which is summarized in the baptismal creed which rightly came into being to express the faith of all called into the Christian fellowship; and which received some metaphysical elaboration for the safeguarding of orthodoxy in the creeds of ecumenical councils, later used at the Eucharist as the Christian equivalent of the National Anthem. In preserving these confessions of faith the Church remains faithful to her continual mandate to proclaim and preserve the kernel of her faith.

In our attempt to reassemble Dr McAdoo's threefold cord of reason, Scripture and tradition as the method of Anglican apologetic, we have so far shown that there is an affinity, even an identity, between the centrepoints or kernels of Scripture and tradition. And this centrepoint of Scripture and tradition is not overshadowed but enhanced by the great variety of setting, language, and imagery which we find in both Scripture and tradition. It remains to be seen, even if briefly, to what extent the third factor 'reason' can be stretched to cohere with the other two: we can do no more than set out the terms on which the threefold synthesis might be reconstructed.

Whatever concept of 'reason' happens to hold the field at any time, theologians of Scripture and tradition should never be content to denigrate or abandon attempts at rational or natural theology, but rather the reverse, unless they are happy to be left talking to themselves in the select language of the Christian tradition. However hard they bang the pulpit or lecture-desk and cry 'Thus saith the Lord', they only utter meaningless noise unless 'the Lord' can be translated or decoded in some intelligible way. Rational theology or theistic metaphysic does not aspire to prove or circumscribe the nature of the living God of the scriptural revelation in its richness and fullness; but it does try to establish some conception of God derived from our experience of the world and of man. Such conceptions of God, we find, are limited by the area of experience from which they start; but they should be able to supply a kind of *praeparatio evangelica*, analogous to the Old Testament, which the Christian revelation and its exponents can address (cf. St Paul's attempt at Athens as presented in Acts 17.23). Along with these concepts we must also include the analogies, images, and metaphors of divine activity drawn from our normal experience.

Even so, if we take revelation seriously, our knowledge of God from other sources can never dictate in advance or limit what is to be revealed. What God reveals must be consistent with all else we know of him, but cannot be constrained by it.

In this essay we have relied heavily on the concept of historical revelation; this in turn must have some rational support. Historical revelation will be supported if we take history seriously, without reducing it to instance, parable, or myth. Each historical action, or each human action in history, is unique, and some are more unique than others: and the Christian faith presents us with Christ as one who is both supremely unique and supremely universal and all-inclusive. Christian theology walks a tightrope, with the ever-present danger of falling to destruction on either side; either so emphasizing the uniqueness of Christ's historic individuality and circumstances as to jeopardize his universal relevance, or so presenting his representative character as to make it seem no more than an instance of a general law or universal myth. But the Christian faith does not see Christ as such an utter paradox, without analogy or parallel; for human history provides examples of individuals who have not only made 'epoch-making' decisions, but also have embodied or represented their class, nation, or creed in remarkable ways. Thus if Christ is understood to be at once a distinctive human individual *and* the representative of the whole human race, this idea is one with many, limited, historical analogies. So we find the earliest Christian thinkers portraying him as the very image of God, the pattern according to which all human nature was created, the true Adam, and the full incarnation of the 'light' immanent in every individual of the species. The rational or 'natural' basis of this will be found in the doctrine of man as made in the image of God, as *capax Dei*, along with such conceptions of human nature as support this doctrine.

We must also reaffirm the divine corollary, the conception of divine grace which does not destroy but perfects and completes human endeavour and action. The divine action does not entirely replace the human, nor act entirely apart from it; indeed, according to the creative plan, it acts alongside and within it. So we find a more general basis for the belief that Christ's intentions and actions are not only integrally human but also divine, a complete expression of the divine mind and will. God was in Christ, reconciling the world to himself, not only by his transcendent wisdom, but also through the conscious and deliberate intention of Christ his instrument and agent. Thus within our broad understanding of religious language there must be a place for positive affirmations with God as their subject. While we agree that 'religious truth' can be conveyed and apprehended by other means, we must accede a special place to the propositions in which Christian truth is enshrined, many of which are classical phrases of holy Scripture, which provide the starting-point, within the New Testament and after the New Testament, for the intellectual, and more than intellectual, enterprise of Christian theology.

Finally, history depends on evidence, and the value of the evidence depends upon the credibility of the witnesses. Merely human witness to Christ is not sufficient, as we have already said; and the Holy Spirit cannot make up for, or supply for, inaccurate or erroneous human witness to human events. But, as we have seen, from the first the Christian tradition included authenticated, corporate testimony to the original saving events. The provision of the gospel of Christ always included provision of witnesses and newsbearers, as St Paul makes clear (Rom. 10.14, 15); and in our reception of the gospel we are not only making an act of faith in the originating Father, and in the effective work of the Son, and in the vivifying of the Spirit, but also in the apostolic body to which it was committed. So it is not inappropriate that the developed forms of the Apostles' and Nicene Creeds include a reference to the Catholic Church as the original and continuous witness to their central truth.

4

G. W. H. Lampe

'Christian life', our report claims, 'is a voyage of discovery.' To 'do theology' is to venture upon an exploration into truth. Yet the Christian believer has no neutral base from which to launch out on his quest, for he is free neither from the prior commitment which his attitude of belief entails nor from the presuppositions implicit in the theological terms in which his faith has hitherto found expression. The very fact that he is a believer means that he stands within a theological tradition embodied in and mediated through the Bible, creeds, liturgy, preaching, the distinctive ethos and outlook of the particular Christian group to which he adheres, and usually, also, the confessional articles of belief of a church.

This is especially true of those who, like myself, have been brought up as church members, baptized in infancy, confirmed as adolescents, and, however much we may have tried to make it our own, inherited rather than personally chose our Christian faith. It applies, however, to all Christians. No one can entirely extricate himself from the complex tradition to which he belongs. He cannot clear the ground and build a new system of belief, using the primary data of revelation as its sole foundation. The believer's exploration into truth cannot set out into uncharted territory. It consists not so much in pioneering as in attempting to analyse, criticize, and evaluate a set of beliefs, and attitudes towards belief, which he has derived from a long stream of tradition, and, where they seem inadequate or misleading as expressions of the faith to which he finds himself committed, to restate, modify, or replace them.

The theological subject-matter for this exploration is furnished from many sources, but its main content comes summarized and focused in catechisms and credal formulations. In the end the whole tradition is a distillation of the experience of our predecessors, and the theologian's, and, indeed, every believer's, voyage of discovery has to proceed in two directions. It must take him into the past in an attempt to appreciate the nature of the experience of those who initiated and developed the characteristic attitudes of Christian faith, and to understand, interpret, and criticize the ways in which their faith and its implications were articulated and expressed in the gradual formation of Christian doctrine. It also has to lead him into an exploration of his own and other people's present experience, and the very difficult and complicated task of investigating how far this present experience confirms and corroborates both the faith of the past and the theology in which it was expressed, how far it can and should be instructed and moulded by what the past has to teach, and how far, on the contrary, present experience is really rendering the past obsolete and requiring that the theological tradition, or even the basic faith which this expressed, should be modified or jettisoned. At every point in this exploration one has to ask the question which Professor Leonard Hodgson asked about the Bible: 'What must the truth have been, and be, if it appeared like that to men who thought and wrote as they did?' Further, since we and our contemporaries are no less subject to the relativities of history than our predecessors were, we have to keep in mind the almost impossibly difficult rider, '. . . and if it appears like this to men who think as we do?'

What we are concerned with is the experience of ourselves and our predecessors, for if divine revelation is given anywhere it is communicated in human experience. The course of our voyage of discovery leads us to try to explore and analyse the sequence: revelation, faith, and theological reflection; possibly also dogmatic formulations of theological reflection such as conciliar definitions, creeds, and articles of belief. Faith is a response to some occurrence, in the broadest sense of that word, which has been experienced as revelatory. It is an attitude of conviction and commitment which may be engendered by experience interpreted as a self-disclosure and self-communication of God. Theological reflection is a process by which this basic attitude of faith—that is to say, belief and trust and other attitudes which are involved in, or consequential upon, belief and trust, such as penitence, obedience, and love—is articulated and interpreted in systems of beliefs and comes to be formulated as 'the Faith'. It might be added that creeds and other theological definitions are summary compendia of the Faith, designed either positively to define the identity of the community which shares this system of beliefs or negatively to exclude those who might claim to belong to this community without in fact subscribing to the Faith as understood by its members. The distinction between the successive terms in the series, revelatory experience, faith, theology, the Faith, is not at all clear-cut, and the precise relationship of the terms to one another is far from easy to establish.

During most of its history the Christian Church has believed itself to be the possessor of a corpus of guaranteed truth in the form of divinely revealed systems of beliefs and theological propositions. It has claimed to be able to use this body of given truth as a criterion to distinguish orthodoxy from heresy. According to this view it was proper to call the doctrine of the Trinity a revealed truth. Unlike the truths that God exists and that the Creator is omnipotent and benevolent, the proposition that God is one substance in three persons expressed a truth which was inaccessible to man's natural reason. It was communicated directly by God, like the proposition that the second person of the Trinity became incarnate for our salvation. Christians have always differed greatly about the content of this body of revealed theological propositions, about where they were to be discovered, whether in the Bible alone or in the Bible together with the continuing tradition of the Church, and about the correct way to interpret them, but they were agreed that truth of this kind existed and had been made accessible; and most Christians have affirmed that in Scripture, credal formulations, conciliar definitions, and to some extent in the writings of the Fathers, or at least in anthologies selected from the works of that rather ill-defined group of theologians, there were to be found revealed doctrines, a divinely authenticated theology.

As I understand the matter, we have come to realize that this is not the case. Theological propositions and systems of belief are not revealed. Theology is a process of reflection on faith that arises from revelatory experience; it is not itself the locus of revelation. That God is one substance in three persons is an hypothesis or model, valuable in so far as, and for so long as, it serves to give an intellectually satisfactory account of the data afforded by revelatory experience, and to articulate and explain the attitudes of faith which are grounded in that experience. It may, indeed, be so valuable as to be indispensable for this purpose; but it is a human theological construction and might in principle prove to have outlived its usefulness. It is not a God-given doctrine, except in the sense in which we may hope and trust that all well-motivated and sincere human thinking in every field of inquiry is divinely inspired and guided. Like the hypothesis of incarnation as a way of theologically articulating the faith-attitude of Christians that is grounded in the revelatory experience of Jesus, it is not an irreformable truth communicated to men by God. This is not to say that there is no such thing as revelation, nor does it mean that there are no criteria for distinguishing good theology from bad. It does, however, imply that our theological expressions of our faith are no more 'revealed' than any other interpretations of our human experience, and that in doing theology we cannot claim to know the whole truth or to have a perfect understanding of such partial truth as we may possess. There is no infallibility available to us.

This breakdown of the concept of revealed theology has been caused largely by the application of historical method to the study of doctrine and by the growth of the comparative study of religion. The great statements of orthodox belief formulated at Nicaea and Chalcedon are seen as products of their time, expressions of what Christians believed about the revelation of God in Jesus in terms of fourth and fifth-century philosophy. They are attempts, conditioned by the world of thought in which their authors lived, including its Greek theological presuppositions, to formulate insights derived from the Bible which had themselves been expressed in the forms of first-century Jewish and Hellenistic thought. They are not timeless expressions of truth communicated from heaven, but human attempts to analyse and describe inferences drawn from men's experience of encounter with God.

It is to this realm of experience that we have to turn in order to discover the locus of revelation. It has often been asserted that divine revelation is given in the events of history. According to this view, God discloses himself and declares his nature and his purposes in human history. In what happens in the affairs of men and nations individuals and communities find themselves addressed by God, encountered by transcendent love, by judgement, acceptance, and forgiveness, and confronted with a sovereign claim and demand for response that involves total commitment, trust, confidence, obedience, and hope. This divine self-disclosure takes the form not of theological propositions, but of 'acts of God' such as the Exodus, Christ's resurrection, and the crises of history which, as the Hebrew prophets believed, manifest his judgement and mercy and calling. The Bible, on this view, is not a source-book for revealed doctrine, but a record of paradigmatic acts of God which serve as a norm and reference-point by which we are enabled to discern God's love and justice and demands elsewhere in the whole course of human history.

Events in themselves, however, even if uninterpreted events were ever accessible to us, would not be revelatory. It is events as interpreted in a particular way which may on certain occasions mediate an encounter between man and God. Events as such do not seem to be divisible into those which are acts of God and those which are not. The Christian may indeed believe that nothing happens which God does not either positively will or at any rate permit, and in this sense all events may be called acts of God; but there seem to be no events which by virtue of some intrinsic quality that distinguishes them from others compel us, whether we are believers or not, to describe them as acts of God. Any event may in certain circumstances lend itself to being so interpreted. No event, on the other hand, need be understood as an act of God in any but the general sense indicated above; in no case is some other interpretation excluded by the observable facts themselves. That this is true is strikingly illustrated by the contradictory interpretations which have been given to the Easter narratives of the appearances of the risen Christ and of the empty tomb, from the disputes recorded by St Matthew to the present-day controversies about such books as Schonfield's *The Passover Plot*. It is also illustrated by the way in which the argument from miracle broke down in early Christian apologetic. It was claimed that Jesus must be the Son of God because he performed miracles which could be accounted for only by acknowledging them to be acts of God. This argument, however, proved unsatisfactory. There always were other theories to account for them. Alternative explanations were available, such as that they were performed by magic akin to that used by sorcerers; and thus the argument came to be reversed. It then ran: 'Jesus is believed, on other grounds, to be the Son of God. If he was the Son of God, it is reasonable to suppose that his works were miraculous acts of God.'

An event, therefore, which for one person may be an act of God need not necessarily be an act of God for someone else; for an act of God is an event which, when interpreted in a particular way, mediates an encounter with transcendent love, beauty, moral judgement, grace, and acceptance: in short, with God's self-communication to man. It is the interpreted event which is the locus of revelation; and the interpretation which makes an event revelatory is derived from the outlook, presuppositions, and habit of mind of the experiencing subject. It is conditioned by particular concepts which he already entertains and by principles of conduct which are traditional for him and upon which he is accustomed to act. This remains true despite the fact that the revelatory experience itself may have a revolutionary effect upon his thinking and his behaviour. The revelatory experience of St Paul on the Damascus road is a case in point. Newman's remarks about scriptural evidences are also relevant here: 'Texts have their illuminating power from the atmosphere of habit, opinion, usage, tradition, through which we see them', so that, 'though a given evidence does not vary in force, the antecedent probability attending it does vary without limit, according to the temper of the mind surveying it'. We are in fact confronted here with a problem which Newman found peculiarly difficult: namely, to distinguish and relate 'external' fact, the impression made by it upon the believing observer, and the theological formulation in which that impression may be articulated and communicated to others. There is a two-way process here which is extremely difficult to analyse. A 'fact' may become revelatory when it is interpreted by an observer in the light of his existing belief, and his belief may already have been formed under the influence of a system of theology. On the other hand, theology is the end-product of a process in which an attitude of faith, that is to say a believing and trusting and obedient response, evoked by revelatory experience, is reflected upon and rationally stated. It seems that faith both results from revelatory experience and also at the same time determines in some measure the revelatory character of the experience by interpreting it as an act of God.

Revelation, then, is never presented to us 'neat' and undiluted. It is communicated to us no more directly in events than, as was formerly supposed, in theological propositions. Nor is revelation given 'neat' in a person, as for instance the person of Jesus Christ; for it is the person as interpreted who may be revelatory for us. The initial interpretation of events, like the subsequent intellectual process of reflection upon them, is conditioned by the human observer and the human situation in which they are experienced. Revelation is never given to us except incarnated in human thought, imagination, and emotion, in the beliefs and values which come to be built up into the tradition of a group, a nation, or a church. There is no possibility of attaching to any event or person a label reading 'guaranteed to be revelatory of God'. What may make us call an event an act of God, or cause us to find God disclosed in it, is our reaction to it, that is to say the effect which it has on us. An event that might in itself be commonplace may disclose whole vistas of truth about ourselves, about other people, and about God's dealings with us.

The Bible is a record of human experience, the interpretations which were placed upon experience, and reflection upon these interpretations. 'God spoke to Moses and said . . .' presumably means in the first instance that Moses thought he was being addressed by God. In his own mind, conditioned as it was by his own past experience and by the traditional beliefs and ethical norms of the people to whom he belonged, and prompted by particular events which were happening, such as the sight of the burning bush (a phenomenon in the external world which can be explained in non-miraculous terms) Moses became convinced that in and through his own thoughts he was being addressed from beyond himself by God's transcendent word. 'Moses thought', or even 'Moses was convinced', are much too weak expressions to describe his experience. Moses was driven to his knees, as we should say, or, as the convention of his time dictated, to remove his shoes, by an overwhelming assurance that God was speaking to him, calling him by name, disclosing himself to him in the mystery and promise of 'I am that I am', and sending him on a mission that he feared would be too hard for him. This was the revelatory experience for Moses. It has been repeated in essence for countless other people in different forms, varying with the temperament and character of the person concerned and his religious, social, and cultural inheritance and environment. Many more people, who have not shared in such a peculiarly vivid and striking experience, have entered sufficiently into the ongoing stream of faith which looks back to Moses' revelatory experience to be able to understand something of its meaning, affirm its truth, and make it a primary influence in their own lives.

Prima facie, however, there is no reason to endorse Moses' belief that God spoke to him any more than the claims made about the Book of Mormon. Ordinary criteria can, nevertheless, be applied to establish whether there is a greater or lesser degree of probability that a particular interpretation of an experience is valid, or, in the language of religious belief, that divine revelation has actually been communicated in an experienced event interpreted in the light of a particular complex of beliefs and presuppositions. Such criteria include the requirement that what is alleged to have been revealed should be consistent and free from self-contradiction, that the content of the supposed revelation should be consonant, or capable of coming to be seen to be consonant, with the general experience of the recipient of the revelation and of those to whom he may communicate it, that it should be in harmony with, and in some measure capable of being verified by, the ongoing human experience of other allegedly revelatory situations, and that its practical effects on the life and conduct of those who accept it as revelation should not be discordant, or should be capable of coming to be recognized as not discordant, with existing belief, grounded in previous revelatory experiences, about God and his dealings with man.

A primary criterion, of course, is whether an alleged revelatory experience is revelatory to me—whether it 'finds me'. But to perceive revelation is rather like appreciating music or painting. 'I know what I like' is a starting-point, but one can be educated by experts, and a wise person will pay attention to the *communis sensus* which has established certain reference-points and recognized some revelatory experiences as 'classical'. This does not mean that one will always be bound by this general opinion; but one will by no means ignore it. In the Christian tradition Christ is the central reference-point and the Bible as a whole contains 'classics' of revelatory experience. By comparison and contrast, again, one person's experience can be related to another's, and what has been seen as revelatory in one religious and cultural tradition can be related to what has been accepted as divine self-disclosure in another; so one can begin to discern coherence, and the criterion for distinguishing true claims to have experienced revelation from false can come to be 'by their fruits you shall know them'.

Criteria of this kind can, of course, only establish probability and not certainty. Nevertheless, they make it possible for us to affirm that the interpretation of certain situations as revelatory seems to be true. In these cases an experience has been interpreted, reflected upon, and acted upon with true insight into its significance and with a proper recognition of an extra dimension of meaning within it, enabling it to be understood as an act of God. Such insight perceives within the human experience such elements as a sense of judgement, graciousness, mercy, claim, demand, calling, and, more generally, an awareness of the reality of things, of transcendence and unexpected depths within the situation, perhaps a glimpse of what Tillich means by 'ultimate concern'. Insight which discerns this dimension, whether in the external events of human history or in the inward experience of the mystic, is what is meant by prophetic inspiration, and inspiration thus appears to be an integral element in revelation.

This element of insight or inspiration may be articulated theologically by means of such concepts as the 'Word' of God that speaks and is heard, and the 'Spirit' of God that illuminates and inspires; and the introduction of these theological terms may perhaps help to counteract the subjectivity of this account of revelation. It is true that what we have, whether at first hand or as reported and handed down in tradition, is the human experience: the experience of a person who claims that God spoke to him. Yet the person concerned is overwhelmingly convinced that it really was God who spoke to him, that he was addressed from beyond himself and encountered by love and grace and beauty which were not generated from his own consciousness, however much his own temperament and his own intellectual, cultural, and social history may have conditioned the form and the manner in which he experienced them. To him the encounter is at least as real and objective as a meeting with a friend. He finds himself compelled to respond by committing himself to nothing less than a basic attitude to life. Even if his response is not at all clearly thought out, it has something in common with the sense of compulsion reflected in the story in the Gospels of the calling of disciples: ' "Follow me", and they got up and followed.' Indeed, some such compulsion is involved in the very interpretation of an event as revelatory. It is an oversimplification to say that the response is evoked by the revelation, for the sense of a compulsion to respond is integral to the experience; it is of its essence, and it makes the occasion revelatory. It seems that we can scarcely avoid the mystery expressed in the conviction that the faith-response is itself a gift of God; and here again we have to introduce such concepts as the 'Word' or 'Spirit' of God illuminating and communicating truth, even though it remains true that the response of faith is always a 'venture' and does not entail intellectual certainty. What it does involve is a readiness to test the validity of a faith-response by making it a principle of action and living by it.

The Bible consists basically of records of, and reflections on, a series of human experiences which were believed by those who narrated the experiences and those who reflected on them to be revelatory of God, disclosures of his personal relations with men in which they were addressed by God's 'Word' and moved by God's 'Spirit', and responded by putting their trust and confidence and hope in God. That this belief was not illusory was confirmed by subsequent experience and reflection. Events continued to be experienced as acts of God, mediating a recognizably similar disclosure of love, grace, and demand and evoking similar faith. On the basis of this continuing experience the faith of the community of Israel was built up and came to be given theological expression. The modes in which divine revelation was encountered were varied, and the development of the community's faith was not uniform, but the central experience of human confrontation with saving love, justice, grace, ethical demand, remains constant and gives an underlying unity to the whole. Reflection on this continuing divine–human relationship of grace and faith produces, by inference, developed theological beliefs, as for instance the 'doctrine' that God who discloses himself in the experienced and interpreted events of human history is the creator on whom the world itself depends for its existence. It is within this stream of experience, faith, and theology, now re-focused around Jesus as presented to us in the New Testament, that we take our place as Christian believers. We belong to the community whose faith is based on broadly this kind of experience and awareness of God. In this sense our faith is biblically based and biblically orientated.

To stand within this tradition, however, does not mean a merely passive acceptance of past insights. Throughout the continuing process of the development of faith and theological reflection the traditional interpretations of experience, and the faith derived from them, have been, and are, subjected to analysis, criticism, and revision in the light of further experience. Thus the Prophets criticized contemporary religious attitudes, and Jesus, while not repudiating the belief that Moses was right in his conviction that God had spoken to him, and therefore not rejecting the system of the Law which had developed out of Israel's reflection on this revelation, radically recast the traditional interpretation of the Law, as also, in a different way, did St Paul. Systems of belief are always subject to processes of change and development. Sometimes these are explicit and drastic, as in the controversies of the Reformation. More often the content of theological concepts and formulations gradually comes to be understood in new ways, even while the language in which it was expressed remains unaltered and creates a deceptive impression that the theology itself is static. Sometimes, again, the theological terms and formulations come almost imperceptibly to be altogether emptied of their original content. An example of changing interpretation might be found in the sense in which we understand the credal clauses about the 'coming again' of Christ and the Judgement. 'He descended into hell' may be an instance of a proposition which has gradually ceased to be meaningful without the aid of antiquarian research into its history.

Changes in theology are not merely a matter of transferring the old wine of faith into new doctrinal bottles. It would be very hard to draw the dividing line where, in this case, wine ends and bottle begins; for theological reflection affects the attitudes of faith which constitute its own subject-matter. Conversely, changed interpretations of revelatory experience, and changed attitudes of faith based upon these, necessarily bring about revisions and modifications of theology and sometimes the discarding of traditional systems of belief. A notable example of the interaction between the faith of believers, their general experience of life and society, and the theology which they profess is to be seen in the radical revision of traditional beliefs about the dispensation by God of rewards and punishments in this life and hereafter. A very prominent idea in the Visitation of the Sick in the Prayer Book was that illness is sent by God as a punishment for sin or a trial of faith. Much traditional thinking, too, about the death of Christ rested on the assumption that to inflict capital punishment, even in the most brutal forms, is entirely right and acceptable provided that it is just, that is, so long as those who are executed are guilty. The rejection of these notions involves much more than a revision of theological formulations; it constitutes a change of attitudes which radically affects the nature of one's basic faith in God.

This process of change can involve the reinterpretation of revelatory experiences themselves. Sometimes they are no longer seen as revelatory, since they appear not to mediate an encounter with God as he has disclosed himself subsequently in other revelations (and especially, for the Christian, in the Pauline 'fruit of the Spirit' which he sees embodied in the character of Jesus). Sometimes, for similar reasons, they may now reveal God in a different, and even contradictory, manner from that which was once supposed. Samuel believed that the incident of Agag disclosed God's authentic will for the total destruction of 'devoted' persons and things, and therefore God's demand for the slaughter of prisoners, and this understanding of that event was incorporated in the faith of Israel. Read in this sense the narrative conveys to me nothing revelatory of God; but it can disclose an aspect of the continuing encounter of man with the 'Word' and 'Spirit' of God, focused for me in the New Testament presentation of Jesus, when it is read in a sense contrary to its original intention: as a disclosure of the evil of inhuman religious fanaticism exemplified in Samuel.

Yet underlying all these processes of change there is a basic continuity: the essentially unchanging human experience of being encountered by God, that awareness of being addressed by a 'Word' of God which, in disclosing transcendent love and goodness and beauty, evokes the sense of divine judgement and forgiveness, and that inspiration and possession by the 'Spirit' of God which creates in the human spirit love, joy, peace, and all those other qualities that are summed up in the Pauline 'fruit of the Spirit'. Through all the discontinuities and fresh developments in both theology and faith human beings continue, in the light of this ongoing experience, to put their trust and confidence and hope in God. At this deep level there is continuity between the people who are now represented for us by the books of the Bible and present-day believers.

The centre and heart of this continuing encounter between God and man is, as I believe, Jesus Christ. In the portrayal in the Gospels of his way of life, focused in his death as the key to the understanding of his life, there is to be found the supreme revelation of the relationship between God and man. Here is the great transforming and redemptive disclosure of God's judgement, compassion, and love; so that the Jesus of the Gospels is God's 'Word' incarnated. Here is also the archetypal pattern of human response to God; it is a total possession by God's 'Spirit', or, in another image, an unbroken relation of 'sonship' to God, expressed in freedom, openness, commitment, and dedication to the love of God, pursued to the point of death. To the Christian believer the Gospels mediate a supremely revelatory experience of God. He finds himself prepared to assert that 'the way things really are', or 'the way the world is made', is focused round this addressing of men by God in Jesus Christ and this compassionate love and the other 'fruit of the Spirit' disclosed in his life and teaching, and in the cross as the central point of disclosure. We Christians, as Professor Baelz has expressed it, 'see in Christ the ground for trusting and hoping in God, the example of trusting and hoping in God, and the source of inspiration and power to trust and hope in God'.

To say this is not to ignore the problem of the extent of our historical knowledge about Jesus. The existence of this problem raises the question how far, if at all, a faith that was originally grounded in a supposedly historical revelatory event can survive if it turns out to be improbable that the event really happened: if, for example, it could somehow be shown to be highly improbable that any Israelites ever did, as a matter of fact, come out of Egypt. The answer would seem to depend on whether the faith which was originally grounded in the Exodus as an actual event (faith, that is to say, in God as 'saviour' and 'redeemer' or a people 'chosen' by his 'grace') was corroborated and confirmed by subsequent experience. If so, then faith in God as saviour and redeemer might find a sufficiently strong empirical basis despite the fact that what had been its original starting-point had turned out to be myth and not history. There seems to be fully adequate support in continuing Christian experience for faith in Jesus Christ as our present 'source of inspiration and power to trust and hope in God', independently of the historicity of an actual resurrection event. This ongoing experience, however, could scarcely be experience of *Jesus Christ* if it were not grounded in the evangelists' picture of him; and it is hardly conceivable that this picture could continue to provide a fully adequate reference-point for subsequent experience of Christ if it could be shown to be totally imaginary.

This point, however, seems somewhat unreal. There does not seem to be good ground for such complete scepticism about the historical existence of a Jesus recognizably like the figure portrayed by the evangelists. It is true that the Gospels are theological compositions in which the traditions about Jesus are skilfully arranged in accordance with the interests and the apologetic, liturgical, homiletic, and other needs of Christians of a later generation. The traditions which they used were themselves embodiments of the reflections of the Church about Jesus in the light of its Easter faith and of a theology which it derived largely from the Old Testament read as an extended prophecy of Jesus' life and death. In the traditions these beliefs and reflections had been retrojected upon the actual figure of Jesus. Nevertheless, although question marks have to be put, for these reasons, against the Gospel picture at all points, there is no necessity to suppose that it is so lacking in historical verisimilitude as to suggest that in fact Jesus was not the sort of person to evoke that faith and give rise to those theological reflections. There is no reason to conclude that he was so essentially different in character from the person portrayed by the synoptists that their portrait has practically no reference to him, or even that he was not the sort of person who could plausibly become the subject of St John's theological reinterpretation.

Christians, however, live not only by a memory but by a vision. The question of the historicity of Jesus is important to us, but the 'Christ' who is the central reference-point of our faith in God is more than the historical Jesus, and 'Christ' belongs to the present more than to the past, and most of all to the future. This truth is vividly presented in the Christian sacraments. Whether or not Jesus himself actually instituted either Baptism or the Eucharist, these sacraments express the continuity of the faith of ourselves today with the central and focal revelation of God that was mediated through the early Christian experience of Christ; and they signify, evoke, and sustain our own experience of living at the present time in the Spirit of Christ. This is an experience of life based on trust and confidence and hope in God whose love and graciousness were disclosed in Christ, life motivated by participation, in some degree, in Jesus' relationship to God (which is summed up in the prayer 'Our Father'), life, too, in which the Christ-like 'fruit of the Spirit' is in some measure reproduced. 'Word' (God's 'address' to us) and 'Spirit' (God's inspiration within us) are continuing present realities, their content being the traditional picture of Christ as seen in the light of the experience of believers in the past and at the present time. Through our experience of God's Spirit presenting Christ to us as the contemporary inspiration and goal of our life we can hope to grow in understanding of truth and awareness of love. The Spirit or 'mind of Christ' can supplement, and even in some respects persuade us to modify, the teaching of Jesus presented to us by the New Testament tradition; and the 'Word' which God addresses to us may be communicated not only through that stream of tradition springing from, and centred upon, the experience and faith described in the Bible, but also through insights derived from revelatory experience in other religious traditions and through disclosures of truth in non-religious experience and thought.

The Christian sacraments also look beyond the present time to a future fulfilment. Christians have always believed that 'Christ' is not simply identical with the Jesus of history. In some sense Christ is still to be fulfilled or completed by his appearance 'in glory'. Christians have expected a 'coming again' of Christ, and on this they have rested their hopes for the future of themselves as individuals, of human society, and of the world itself. We may perhaps envisage the fulfilment of this hope as the completion of the transformation of mankind by God's Spirit reproducing or re-presenting in human beings that 'sonship' to God and that 'fruit of the Spirit' which pre-eminently characterized Jesus, so that in the end they will truly reflect Christ. Christ will thus be glorified in Christ-like humanity, or, as others such as V. Lossky have envisaged it, the Spirit of God will be hypostatized in the saints; and when the human race is manifested as being 'sons of God', as St Paul says in Romans 8.19–23, the effect on the rest of the world, so long exploited and oppressed by mankind, will be no less than liberation and renewal.

As a Christian believer I conceive myself to be part of this continuing stream of faith and hope which responds to revelatory experience, and I align myself with the general intention and direction of the theological tradition built up in the past by those who have attempted to give a rational account of this faith and hope. I do not think that believers today are necessarily committed to the forms in which this theological interpretation of our faith was expressed in the past. The fourth and fifth-century creeds, like the sixteenth-century confessions, tried to give

contemporary answers to questions which were then contemporary
We do not ask the same questions today, and we cannot simply repeat
their answers in reply to the different questions of our time, though we
may well think that in their day the creeds and confessions were right as
against their opponents. Some of their formulations, as for instance, in
my view, the credal clause 'Born of the Virgin Mary', or the fourth
Anglican Article, 'Of the Resurrection of Christ', are now misleading
statements. They can, indeed, be understood as signifying, among other
things, the reality of Christ's humanity (he was truly born into this
world of human beings) together with the recognition that with his birth
a fresh divine initiative changed the course of human history, and the
continuity of the present and future Lord with the Jesus of history; but
these valuable theological ideas are now obscured by being presented in
the form of statements which, taken at their face value, I hold to be
untrue.

The historic creeds, however, and to a considerable extent the
sixteenth-century confessions such as the Thirty-Nine Articles,
continue to mark out areas in which vitally important questions arise
which the believer of the twentieth or any other century cannot afford to
ignore but with which he must somehow come to terms if his faith is to
be coherent and intelligible. The function of the creeds is less to give us
answers to repeat than to remind us of questions which we must keep on
asking.

Nevertheless, as Christian believers we continue to want to assert
that human experience points to God as the creator of all things, despite
the great problem of evil of which the creeds remind us when they speak
of God as being both 'Father Almighty' and also 'Maker of heaven and
earth'. We want to affirm that the life and death of Jesus is the focal
point of our encounter with God's compassionate, redemptive, and
transforming love; that God's 'Word' and 'Spirit' which were supremely
disclosed to men in the evangelists' presentation of Jesus continue to
encounter us today; that Christ will 'appear in glory' when his Spirit is
reflected in a transformed world; that in the meantime there is a
community, to which we belong, where Christlikeness, the 'fruit of the
Spirit', is reproduced in some measure by divine grace answered by
faith and where we can participate in the experience of past and present
believers and hope for that perfection of communion with God which
we call eternal life. In making affirmations of this kind we are sharing
the intention of the framers of the creeds even though we have discarded
the concepts of revelation and authority with which they operated.

5

H. E. W. Turner

To attempt to state a theological position within the limit of five thousand words is a formidable undertaking. It is bound to omit much, not least the rough working by which conclusions are reached, and therefore to sound more dogmatic than it is meant to be.

As the Christian life can best be understood as a responsive dependence upon God, so Christian theology must be approached from the standpoint of the divine givenness. This is not wholly inconsistent with an element of adventure, openness, or exploration but leads to a different approach to theology and an end-product which may well appear less open-ended or exciting. All would agree that Christian theology cannot dispense with faith which on the basis of insights into God can lead to a degree of certitude practically indistinguishable from knowledge. Any theology requires a framework of thought and the use of categories which will not secure universal acceptance and involve value-judgements which not everyone will share.

This paper will make certain assumptions. God has revealed himself to men in history in various ways and different manners. Despite its differences in literary form and cultural contexts, the Bible has a definite cognitive content from which the task of theology starts and to which it must remain faithful. Theology can organize, codify, and draw inferences from it; it can never desert or modify the biblical data. The Bible remains the basic norm for Christian theology, for it contains not only the record of human search and discovery but also a divine self-disclosure in deed as God revealed himself progressively to man in history and in word as the record of the events which together make up the fabric of salvation history. It contains insights into God and information about his being and character, his actions and purposes which are not available from any other source, and it is still a place of encounter where God meets with man. A second norm for theology is to be found in the catholic creeds, especially the Apostles' and Nicene Creeds. These are alike a true reflection of the essentials of the Christian gospel and the product of the collective thinking of the Church during the classical formative period of theology. They set the guidelines for later theological thought. Their universal acceptance by the historic churches supplements their intrinsic authority and their abandonment as norms or guidelines for theological thinking by any part of the Church would impair its loyalty to truth, constitute a serious break with Christian history and a grave weakening of the bond of Catholic 'togetherness'. They do not, however, exclude further thought on the topics which they contain or the attempt to translate them into different categories, provided that the emphases and balance of the traditional faith is not thereby weakened or altered. Loyalty to the creeds is not, for example, satisfied by claiming that we ought to think out the problems of theology afresh in our own day as they attempted to do in theirs without regard to the question whether it is the same gospel that we are presenting and the same faith that is being set forth.

The givenness of God implies both his transcendence and immanence, for what God does he antecedently is. This means that we cannot avoid ontological categories in the doctrine of God, provided that they are qualified by some technique like analogical predication. Even the traditional use of negative metaphysical adjectives with regard to God, such as invisible, immutable, and impassible, is defensible both as the attempt to deny creaturely limitations to God and as pointing in negative form to his fullness of being. Ontology supplies the least inadequate way of describing God, provided that its constructions are not regarded as a conceptual photograph of God. What has been disparagingly called the supernaturalist frame seems quite indispensable to any theology which seeks to maintain divine transcendence and self-existence at anything like their full strength. The spatial language which has often been used to discredit it is more a way of talking, natural and perhaps inevitable to space-ridden man, than a valid objection to what it seeks to convey. To accept this framework and to start our theology, as it were, from above, does justice, as nothing else can, to the divine priority and prevenience in revelation and action. While historically the doctrine of the Trinity can be seen as an extended theological inference from the New Testament data about Christ and the Holy Spirit, it is also intended as a statement about God as he is in himself and not as a mere description of the way in which he has acted towards man. An Immanent or Essential Trinitarianism is therefore a more adequate doctrine than an Economic doctrine of the Trinity. As the Scholastics put it, operation follows Being, and cannot therefore merely be substituted for it. In its classical form the doctrine of the Trinity claims that we can apprehend God as he really is without the further impertinence of asserting that we comprehend him fully. On the basis of revelation and the divine action recorded in the Bible we can say as much as this, while recognizing that the being of God ultimately far surpasses human thought and language. The doctrine of the Trinity falls between a heaven-assailing gnosticism and a timorous agnosticism which dares not push the data of revelation and human thought about them as far as they will carry us. The doctrine of the Trinity is highly evocative of worship and adoration, but this claim depends completely upon the truth of the doctrine as the best exploration of the data of revelation and the closest approximation to the inner being of God which Christians can attain.

The immanence of God describes his activity in and in relation to creation. This is not a matter of moral or metaphysical necessity, but an act of grace which is fully congruous with God's nature as love. As William Temple pointed out, God would be God without the world; the world without God would be nothing at all. It represents the paradox of the 'overspill' of the divine love which passes and repasses from eternity to eternity within the Holy Trinity 'For ever full, for ever shared, a never-ending sea', and yet finds its expression in a created order. The doctrine of creation is both a statement about origins and an assertion of the continuing dependence of the universe upon God. Creation and preservation belong inseparably to each other but are not identical. The method of creation appears to be by evolution, whereby the universe, without ceasing to be dependent upon God, is given a real place in its own development. For a theologian the scientific account of evolution is description and not explanation. Science can neither deny nor assert what a scientist has called 'a transcendental singularity occurring when t (Time) equals O', nor the presence or absence of a divine will immanent within the process. Theology on its part is free to assert that the explanation of the evolutionary universe is to be found in the prior being and active will of God. But God is neither simply the 'unmoved mover', a principle of logical explanation with no further contact with or interest in his universe (deism), nor simply an immanent principle within the universe with no independent existence of his own (pantheism).

If divine transcendence grounds divine immanence in the prior being of God, immanence begins to spell out the active will of God in his dealings with the universe. It is a graduated givenness corresponding to a graded World Order. The will of God, absolute in itself, leaves adequate living space for the reality of secondary or created causes. Within the universe the immanence of God is adapted to the capacity of creatures to receive it.

Within this graded universe there is the possibility of the emergence of 'genuine novelties' such as man which are 'novelties' in respect of the process while yet remaining within the process. The style or idiom of divine immanence varies from what looks like 'general assent' at the level of atoms and molecules to the level of man where creation can rise to the free obedience of sons or sink to the determined resistance of disobedient rebels. The biblical story of the Fall expresses the state of disobedience, estrangement, and fallenness which is the environment (and perhaps the heredity) of natural man. By whatever means, in the course of human history mankind has come to issue a Unilateral Declaration of Independence from God with dire results. There is a solidarity in Adam which is a solidarity in sin. The image of God in man, of which the writer of Genesis speaks, is defaced, though not completely effaced or obliterated.

For the Christian theologian the history and religion of Israel has a continuing significance. Here is embodied in a single case history of sufficient duration and cultural diversity an adequate test-case for the dealings of God with man. The small geographical scale on which the affairs of the nation were conducted, their relative insignificance politically, economically, and even culturally only serve to emphasize the theological importance of the People of God. From one point of view the Old Testament is the record alike of God's continual quest for his people and their response to him. It is a book of the call of God both in speech (revelation) and act (salvation-history), in mercy and judgement. It is also a book of man's response to God, at best patchy, at worst blind and defiant. The special nature of God's dealings with Israel does not, of course, imply his absence from, or lack of interest in, the human race elsewhere.

This sets the stage for the incarnation, and the background against which it is best approached. It is decisive and unique, but it was prepared for within the history of Israel and took place in a particular historical and cultural context. Its background is divine immanence in creation, but the incarnation cannot be reduced to a special case of divine immanence. Since a full and perfect human nature is involved, it can be described as a genuine 'novelty' within the process but it is not explicable solely by reference to the process. The incarnation involves a divine descent into the world. The New Testament language about pre-existence cannot be explained as a specially striking way of expressing the 'importance' of Christ as the predestinate man, the man of God's own choosing, but neither does it mean that Jesus himself pre-existed. While historically pre-existence was an inference from the continuing presence and existence of Christ after the resurrection, it marks the transition (itself a matter of revelation) in the belief and understanding of the primitive Church from Jesus the Son of God to God the Son expounded in terms of the Wisdom and the Word or Logos in the New Testament, which anchors the incarnation firmly in the antecedent being of God. It is a question not of experience but of revelation. The incarnation involves the paradox that God the Son came as a stranger to a world to which he was already no stranger. As the doctrine of the cosmic Christ in the Epistles to the Colossians and Ephesians, the Epistle to the Hebrews, and the Prologue to the Fourth Gospel reminds us, the Logos who became incarnate in Christ participated in the divine act of creation. 'He came to his own and his own received him not.' Its purpose was a rescue operation mounted at utmost cost by God for the redemption of the world, 'for us men and for our salvation'. The shocking nature of the paradox is described as the 'Word made flesh'. God the Son, 'of one substance with the Father', is fully and personally involved, and yet a full and complete humanity is also involved. This double solidarity of our Lord both with the Father and with ourselves implies the classical doctrine of the two natures if its conditions are even approximately to be met. The union of both in a single Person who is both divine and human is the theological problem to which the mystery of the incarnation gives rise. It is not surprising that the would-be christologian finds himself walking a tight-rope and that over-simplification is perilous. An approach to Christology from the side of God alone might lead to an unreal or even a fictional humanity. An approach too exclusively from the side of man might lead to moral unity or unity in activity and fail to provide a unity of Person within the incarnate Lord. If God the Son were not the ultimate subject of the incarnate life, divine solidarity and divine involvement would be 'sold short'. If he had not assumed a full and complete humanity, his act of redemption would fail in relevance and his solidarity with us be impaired. As in revelation God speaks to man as man can hear and receive, so in the incarnation God meets man where he is, and rescues him from the predicament arising from human sin. In the words of St Irenaeus, 'He came not as he could but as we could bear.' The resources of human thought and language are not adequate to the central mystery of the incarnation. That is no excuse either for evading the christological task or settling for an oversimplification of its problems. In constructing a Christology to succeed is not to fail too badly. The incarnation as a saving fact stands fast; its manner remains a mystery in the positive sense of an act which passes human understanding. It is not a logical puzzle which hurts the mind but a genuine mystery which liberates the spirit. We must take rational trouble over the mystery, while avoiding oversimplifications which iron out the paradox or reduce the mystery. This does not amount to the murder of logic, still less of theology, but a recognition of the necessary limits both of logic and theology in handling the unique union of natures divine and human in which God the Son is the ultimate subject.

The focal point then both in religion and theology is the incarnate Lord. The Jesus of the Gospels is the Way, the Truth, and the Life. He is our clue both to the character of God and the meaning of man. The Virgin Birth (or more correctly the Virginal Conception), considered as an event within history, differentiates the Word made flesh from the birth of an ordinary, individual man. Though the evidence is of a different historical texture from 'suffered under Pontius Pilate', it appears to me sufficient to support this conclusion. Although the Empty Tomb is not the only strand in the evidence for the resurrection, it is an early and inescapable part of the evidence as a whole. Taken together the Virgin Birth and the Empty Tomb set the boundary limits of the incarnate life which lies between them. The miracles depend upon the mystery, not the mystery upon the miracles. They are in act what the words at the baptism and the transfiguration are in speech: 'This is my Beloved Son in whom I am well pleased; hear him.' The Descent into Hell (or Hades) is scantily evidenced in the New Testament, but has a twofold important reference. If taken exclusively with 'suffered, dead and buried' it emphasizes still further the reality of the human sufferings and death of Christ, but it may also contain a further allusion to Christ's victory over death by dying, making available the new life and the 'larger hope' at least to those who had died in hope, not having obtained the promises. The meaning of the ascension is not exhausted by the assertion of a physical levitation of the risen Christ from the earth in which no doubt St Luke himself believed. It is the last post-resurrection appearance of Christ recognized by his disciples to be the last and marks his return to the glory which was his as God the Son with the Father from eternity. The Feast of the Ascension is the Festival of Christ the King. The Second Coming of Christ is awaited by the Church at the consummation of history as a happening in which the one who participated in the divine act of creation, who was made man for us men and for our salvation, will be manifested as the mediator of divine judgement as he is now the bringer of God's salvation and mercy. The extended second article of the creed concentrates upon the incarnation as the decisive act in salvation-history. We miss its intention completely if we expect a mention of the teaching and life-style of Jesus. For this the Church directs us to the Gospels.

The question has been raised whether the centre of gravity in Christianity is to be found in God or in Christ. In this form the question is an unreal one. A strong emphasis on the centrality of Christ is not inconsistent with, and even demands, a strong doctrine of God, while a strong doctrine of God is not inconsistent with a fervent devotion to Christ and a high Christology. Neither of the two main classical traditions in the Church of England has found any difficulty in combining both. Yet, partly as a protest against what Karl Barth called 'Jesuism' and partly as a result of some radical tendencies in New Testament criticism, there has begun to be talk about a 'false Christo-centrism'. True a theological judgement on the significance of Christ cannot solve critical questions at a stroke or determine in advance what answers are acceptable. But there is no doubt that some conclusions, and even more some occasional statements, which (given their context) are perhaps not to be taken too seriously, cause considerable pain and shock to others who cannot rightly be accused of timidity or lack of honesty. For them much more is at stake than their partners in dialogue appear to realize. It is common ground that the study of historical documents is attended by historical risk and, except in a minority of cases, certainty must be replaced as our criterion by probability. Yet we cannot remain indifferent to questions of probability. Admittedly the older quest for the historical Jesus has been killed stone dead. This does not mean the search for historically probable conclusions is fruitless or that its results may not have great importance both for theology and religion. The present impasse is partly due to the type of questions which are being asked of the Gospels. While the defect of the older criticism was to try to elbow out the Church to get at the 'nuclear Jesus', the opposite tendency to discover the Church everywhere without a parallel concern for the Gospels as historical evidence about Jesus is equally onesided. If we cannot see Jesus historically except through documents compiled within the Church and for its use, it is equally true that the Gospels are witnesses to Christ and embody the Church's 'remembrance' of Jesus. Their ultimate subject is Jesus and not the Church. Nor will it do, as in some forms of catholic modernism, to switch the emphasis from Christ to the Church as though this could be an adequate theological or religious substitute. The centrality of Christ remains the distinctive feature of Christianity among the world-faiths. This must not be weakened or obscured. This is the message of the New Testament, and to it the creeds point in their extended second article.

The Holy Spirit who 'proceeds from the Father and the Son' and who 'with the Father and the Son together is worshipped and glorified' is fully God within the eternal Trinity. He participates in the operations of the Father and the Son (for there are no 'blank files' within the triune God), but he does not bear witness of himself. As the Lord and the Lifegiver, he is God's sign-manual within the created order, certifying it as God's creation. He is the principle of divine immanence in the universe. His action, whether recognized or not, lies behind the quest for truth and thereby justifies Christians in claiming all truth for Christ. His inspiration makes men fitted to be vehicles of divine revelation. He initiates and enables man's response to God, and in particular he takes the things of Christ and shows them to the Church. He is not absent from the incarnation of Christ. In the Pauline Epistles to be 'in Christ' and to be 'in the Spirit' are overlapping concepts. Indeed in the New Testament there is an overlap between the risen Christ and the Holy Spirit though it never reaches the point of strict identification. It may be suggested that, while the concept of the Spirit helped to explain the ubiquity of the risen Christ, its association with him assisted the development of the Old Testament idea of the Spirit as an activity or a force towards a fuller notion of personality. Above all, through the outpouring of Pentecost, he is closely associated with the life of the Church. It would, however, be wrong to restrict his presence and guidance within the Church to its more spectacular manifestations. He should not (in the words of John Mackay) be made the patron of ardour against order. The Church as the Body of Christ is alike the symbol (expression) and the instrument of Christ. During its earthly ministry its instrumental character will always be more pronounced. The Church cannot properly be called the extension of the incarnation because it is always unilaterally dependent upon Christ. If, as Calvin noted in his comment on 1 Corinthians 12.10, St Paul can call the Church Christ, the proposition cannot be reversed. That is the error of some forms of catholic modernism which seek to replace the centrality of Christ by the 'importance' of the Church, as well as of an ecclesiological particularism which restricts the limits of the Church unduly. Christ is both Lord in the Church and Lord over the Church in judgement as well as in mercy. That is why a recall from the Church to Christ may become necessary as at the Reformation and conceivably in other circumstances. The Church has many aspects and dimensions. It is both human and divine, human because it is composed of sinners like ourselves, divine in its calling and foundation and as the place where God in Christ encounters and brings grace to man through the operation of the Holy Spirit. To take either aspect apart from the other would lead to theological disaster, either to a false ecclesiastical perfectionism (what St Augustine called the angelic fallacy) on the one hand, or a reduction of the Church to the status of a particular, even a peculiar, type of social organization on the other. It has both visible and invisible characters, and once again this can lead to exaggeration if either is stressed at the expense of the other. The true Church is not merely an invisible Communion of Saints known only to God and dispersed throughout the empirical churches or, even more dangerous, a Church of the Saints composed of former members called out of the empirical churches. The Church belongs to the three dimensions of time. It belongs to the past since it is firmly grounded on the Bible and the creeds. It is called to live, serve, and witness in the present. It looks forward in the future to its fulfilment in the Communion of Saints and the life of the world to come.

It is not therefore surprising that tension may arise between its loyalty to the past and its witness in the present and that different policies may be recommended to handle it. Freedom, adventure, openness on the one hand are matched by loyalty, obedience, and responsive dependence on the other. Each word would need careful analysis if we are not to be trapped in a theological 'double-think'. For myself I am convinced that the Church has norms of belief and teaching, first and foremost the Bible, but also the historic creeds as subordinate or dependent standards. The freedom of the Church is qualified by its loyalty; its adventure of faith falls within the divine givenness. Its openness is first and foremost an openness to God. The Church must hold fast to the past if it is not to become a society without roots, yet it must always seek to remain within earshot of its own contemporaries. Sometimes the best service which it can render is to hold fast to the abiding truth of the faith and the full message of the gospel. There may well be a danger of teaching another faith or proclaiming another gospel. By oversight restatement may become understatement and the gospel restricted not to what each generation must hear but to what we believe that they will accept. Due regard ought certainly to be paid to honest minds and tender consciences of those who do not or cannot as yet accept the full content of the creeds but this cannot be at the expense of the corporate loyalty of the Church to the Bible and the creeds. Any weakening here would involve both a breach with our historical position in matters of doctrine and with other churches with whom we are moving towards closer relations. The silent majority of our own people has rights against, as well as duties towards, an articulate minority, however questing their minds and honourable their intentions.

6

M. F. Wiles

In our joint report we have tried to do justice to the place of adventure and exploration in Christian faith and also to that of a given tradition. There is a great deal that man does not and cannot know; but he does not simply have to start from scratch with nothing better than his own individual experiences or ideas to go on. On the absolute necessity of both inquiry and tradition we are all agreed. But we differ in the weight different members give to each aspect. I stand somewhere in that part of the spectrum which stresses the questioning and exploratory character of Christian faith. But I am none the less convinced that such exploration is not likely to be of much value unless it takes the past tradition of Christian belief—and in particular its expression in Scripture and creeds—very seriously. Not a few suggested restatements of Christian belief in our own time seem to me to be unsatisfactory very largely because they fail to do this. But once one allows the need for both these elements—exploration and tradition—it follows that the belief patterns that will emerge from equally honest and competent attempts to bring the two together are bound to differ. We ought not to expect identical results, even from those who approach Christian belief in essentially the same spirit. In this paper, then, I shall speak entirely personally and try to give some account of what Christian belief is like for me as I try to formulate it and to make it a basis of life in the kind of way that our report has set out to describe.

Fundamental to any religious belief is its understanding of God. Christian faith has been especially distinguished from other faiths by the trinitarian character of its affirmations about God. I propose to take this as the starting-point of what I want to say, partly because it is so fundamental but also because it illustrates both the negative and the positive aspects that are bound to figure in any questioning response to the tradition that comes to us from the past.

When in the early centuries the Church developed its distinctive account of God as one in three persons, it always insisted that its language was woefully inadequate for the reality it was seeking to express. We use the word 'persons', Augustine said in effect, not because it is a satisfactory word, but because the only alternative is a silence which leaves the way open to even more misleading conceptions. But despite this stress on the inadequacy of the language and the mysterious nature of the reality of which they were trying to speak, they also insisted that they were not simply describing the way we experience God or the way he appears to us but that they were making an affirmation about the nature of God himself. Much of my professional life as a scholar has been concerned with historical study of how that trinitarian form of faith arose in those early centuries of the Christian era. I think I can see why the Church came to such a belief, given the culture and philosophical conditions of the time. With many (though not all) of the things that drove them to formulate their beliefs that way I am in basic sympathy. I certainly believe that there is one God whose being is infinitely rich and complex, but given the culture and philosophical conditions of our own time—and accepting them, I hope, not slavishly but critically—I do not believe that it is possible for us to claim that kind of precise knowledge (however mysterious) about the nature of God in himself.

Language about God, as we have emphasized in our report, is necessarily indirect—even poetic in character, a word with which I am much less unhappy than the report as a whole. But the philosophy in terms of which they were working and the way of viewing Scripture that was universally accepted at the time are very different from those which would characterize the work of almost any theologian today. I cannot with integrity say that I believe God to be one in three persons. My questioning—historical and philosophical—does not leave me with sufficient grounds to form a belief on such a question one way or the other. But I am happy to accept such language from the tradition as a vehicle of worship and of thinking about God, because much of what lies behind it seems to me to embody things of vital importance for Christian faith today.

What then are those things?

'I believe in God the Father Almighty, Maker of heaven and earth.' The first clause of the creed is not a primary issue of debate or controversy within the Church. But this should not lead us to treat it either as something self-evident or as mere introduction to all that follows. It was certainly not self-evident to people at the time when the creeds were being formed. Although there was no atheism and little agnosticism in the sense that we know them today, the gods in whom most people believed were limited either in their benevolence or in their control over, and responsibility for, the world. How could the world as we know it with all its suffering and evil be the product of a God who was both wholly good and all-powerful? The early Church was well aware of the problem, and no sensitive Christian can fail to be so today. But recognizing the reality of the problem the Church still expressed its fundamental faith in a God who was wholly good, wholly in control of, and wholly responsible for, the world. And that faith has been basic to the Christian tradition ever since. That is the faith that is handed down to us. For me it is equally fundamental, not simply because it is so handed down, but also because for me too nothing else corresponds as adequately to reflection on the wonder of the world's existence, its mysterious nature and the profundities of men's moral and spiritual experience. But it remains a faith and a hope. The problem of evil does not just go away. It is still at hand as counter-evidence, so that the Christian's faith, like Job's, has to be held in spite of it and through it.

Such a faith is not just a theoretical matter. It has consequences for our basic attitude towards the world. It implies an attitude of ultimate confidence about the world, that does not simply ignore but can never finally be overwhelmed by the many things that seem to make such an attitude unreasonable. It implies a positive attitude to the created order, but one that has an element of detachment saving us from enslavement to its demands. Faith in God is not just a decision to adopt such an attitude to the world, it is the ground and reason for it.

In the past men have often thought to see evidence for this goodness and power of God in events which embodied his special and miraculous working on behalf of his people. Miracle stories figure prominently throughout the Bible and providential answers to prayer are a characteristic feature of much popular Christian piety. In general I am unconvinced by such stories and the interpretations given of them. I do not think we are given such specific signs of God's goodness or God's power as they suggest. The New Testament's warning against dependence upon miraculous signs needs to be taken very seriously. We live by faith and not by sight. There is a hiddenness about God's goodness and his power which means that faith can never be made secure beyond a peradventure. But faith without any evidence would be nothing but foolish credulity. The kind of faith in God of which I have been speaking needs more grounding and more body than is forthcoming from purely general experience and reflection on the world as a whole. For me such further grounding and body are focused on the person of Jesus. What then is the nature of my beliefs about him?

And in Jesus Christ, his only Son our Lord . . .'. The second and longest clause of the Apostles' Creed shows the centrality of faith in Jesus Christ for Christian belief. The way in which it is set out there sometimes gives the impression that this is an item of belief, clearly distinct and separable from that of the belief in God the Father affirmed in the first clause of the creed. But any such way of thinking is untrue to the trinitarian character of Christian faith. It is one God in whom the Christian is believing when he believes in the Father and in the Son. So for me faith in Jesus Christ as God's only Son is first and foremost a characterization of my faith in God. It gives expression to the conviction I have already indicated, namely that if my faith in God is to have shape, form, and content—as any religious faith must do—then the primary source for that shape must be the tradition that derives from, and centres upon, Jesus. It is there that I must turn for the most reliable understanding of the nature and purposes of God and in search of the spiritual power to realize those purposes in life.

But the creed, of course, spells out what is involved in faith in Jesus Christ in more specific terms, as is appropriate if the role of such faith is to give more definite shape to our general faith in God. The kinds of affirmation that it makes about Jesus fall into three main groups. At one extreme there are essentially metaphysical claims about his person: he is God's only Son (or, more fully in the Nicene Creed, 'of one substance with the Father'). At the other extreme are straightforward historical statements of a kind which might apply to anyone: 'suffered under Pontius Pilate, was crucified, dead, and buried'. But in between these two extremes are various statements, which in differing ways have, or seem to have, some sort of rooting in history but are not just straightforward historical claims: 'conceived by the Holy Ghost, born of the Virgin Mary . . . the third day he rose again from the dead, he ascended into heaven, and sitteth on the right hand of God the Father Almighty, from whence he shall come again to judge both the quick and the dead'. And here again the Nicene Creed adds the important further concept that these things happened through his coming down from heaven 'for us men and for our salvation'.

About the first class—the more metaphysical beliefs—I have to say the same as I said about the belief in God as one in three persons. My historical studies help me to understand how and why the Church came to speak in such terms in the early centuries—and in large measure to respect its judgement in doing so. But my sense of the limitations of all human knowledge in such spheres makes me stress that in using such language myself I am necessarily using language in a very indirect, even poetic, way to express the central role of Jesus in giving form and life to our faith in God.

The second class presents no special problem. It is clear—and it is something that the Church has always insisted on—that Jesus was fully human. His suffering, death, and burial were as real as the suffering, death, and burial of any other man.

Statements in the third group are more difficult and really should be dealt with separately, if space allowed. In none of these cases, where there is an historical reference, are we in a position to judge with any confidence what exactly happened. They are for the most part beliefs that have roots in the history of Jesus, in his teaching and in what happened. But they are expressed in a way which draws imaginatively on a wide range of religious symbolism and aspiration. Treat them as a series of isolable facts about Jesus of Nazareth and I would have to express myself puzzled and uncertain about most of them. But see them as expressive of the transforming power and significance of the figure of Jesus in human life, and I respond to them differently. For they speak of a conviction that by the grace of God sin and death have been and can be overcome in human life, a conviction made possible for the man whose faith in God is informed by what he finds in the figure of Jesus.

'I believe in the Holy Ghost . . .'. My approach to this affirmation of belief in the third person of the Trinity is similar to my approach to the second person. In this case such an approach probably fits rather better with the way in which very many Christians feel about this element in their creed. People not uncommonly have a feeling of guilt that they are unable in practice to conceive the Holy Spirit as a 'person' of the Godhead in the way that they perhaps do feel able to do in the case of the Son. I do not think there is any cause to feel guilt about such a failure. Here too we have to do with an essential element in the characterization of Christian belief in God. God is not simply the hidden source of our being; nor are his nature and purposes given shape solely through reflection on that which is revealed in the history of Jesus. Man's relationship to God is more intimate and more contemporary than that description would do justice to. The emergence of Christian belief in the Holy Spirit was grounded in the early Church's experience of the transforming power over human life that they discovered in their fellowship in the name of Jesus, their risen Lord. Belief in the Spirit is belief that that transformation is still possible—in ways as little expected and as little under our constraint as it was for the early Church.

How God is at work in such transformations of human life I do not claim to understand—in any case we understand very little about the inner springs of personal life in general. For myself I wish to be as chary of claims that specific insights or achievements are the immediate result of the Holy Spirit's working as I am about God's miraculous intervention or providential ordering of particular events in the natural world. My basic conviction is that where men are open to God in the life of faith, God's eternal purpose for the enhancement of personal life can be and is made effective in their lives. Holiness is not primarily an outcome of stern moral endeavour but rather of such an openness to God. In terms of doctrine and belief, faith in the Holy Spirit is the conviction that the adventure and exploration of which we have tried to speak in our report is justified and can be a medium by which God enables us to discover new aspects of the truth.

So far I have been speaking almost entirely about beliefs, about the definition in words of the specific content of Christian faith. It seemed a natural thing to do because I was particularly concerned with the relation of Christian faith today to its expression in the historic creeds. Yet it has also been a somewhat paradoxical emphasis to make, because an important part of what I have wanted to stress has been the impossibility of giving a clear and precise verbal form to that content. The development of both historical and philosophical study seems to me to militate against the possibility. If the definition of belief were central to Christian faith that would be a profoundly worrying phenomenon. But faith is not just intellectual assent to a series of belief statements about God and Jesus. It is a response of the whole person to the ultimate reality of the world, as apprehended through Jesus and the tradition springing from him. It has an intellectual side to it and the relative importance of that aspect will vary for different individuals in their religious faith, as in other areas of life the role of the intellect varies for different people.

What is important for the Christian community at large is not that it gets its beliefs absolutely clear and definite; it cannot hope to do that if they are really beliefs about God. It is rather that people within the community go on working at the intellectual problems, questioning, testing, developing, and seeking the practical application of the traditions that we have inherited from the past.

But for all its insistence that the intellect is not all important, does that account not still suggest a picture of Christianity which is more like a philosophers' discussion group than a house of faith? I do not believe that it does. For the life of faith is shaped not by a set of clear-cut beliefs, but by a whole rich tradition of imagery, of worship, and of patterns of life and conduct. It is these that provide the assurance, the deepening, and the direction that man needs. They kindle the imagination so that he can find a deeper and richer meaning in the ordinary experience of life and they provide the medium through which he can direct himself towards, and open himself to, that love, which is life's source and goal. None of these features of the tradition is fixed and unchangeable, but nor are they indefinitely flexible. The tradition has a shape and a character and so can give shape and character to man's response to God. Throughout its history the Church has kept on trying to give to its tradition a more permanent and more unchanging character. It has been right, as I have already said, to go on working in this kind of way at the intellectual issues implicit in its faith and life. But to claim permanence for any of its specific achievements in this field runs the risk of constituting a form of the sin of idolatry. For what lies behind it may be a seeking for ultimate security not in God but in the medium through which we have our relationship with him. Thus the way of faith involves a combination of receptivity and criticism. It involves living with a tradition, allowing its riches to feed the imagination and the spirit, to correct our prejudices, and to enlarge our sympathies beyond the narrow range of our immediate experience. But it involves doing so critically. The tradition criticizes us, but we have also to criticize the tradition, drawing upon the best intellectual and moral insights of our own day.

I have spoken in very general terms of the need to be receptive but critical in relation to the tradition. I have stressed the need to see it in its various forms as the medium through which a relationship with God is made possible, yet never to give to it the absolute position that belongs to God alone. Something very like that was, I believe, characteristic of Jesus himself. And there we see it, not in abstract terms but in the concrete form that is vital for faith. For Jesus stood firmly in the tradition of Jewish faith, but handled that tradition with a freedom that sometimes shocked his contemporaries. And he was particularly critical of those who absolutized the tradition and so were unable to recognize what God was saying to them and doing with them in their own day. In this way Jesus is the model and the inspiration of the man of faith.

But he is more than that. It is through him, as I have already said, that we are enabled to give fuller substance to what would otherwise be a very inchoate form of belief in God. And the heart of that fuller substance is the absolute identification with the other, the perfect self-giving in love which the story of the incarnation, the redemptive understanding of his death, and the proclamation of his triumphant resurrection so vividly depict. For they do it in a way which by its imaginative form is able to call out our love and enter into the formation of our lives at the deepest level of our beings.

I have spoken of a *story* and of its *imaginative* form, not because I regard them as mere human inventions. I do so rather because neither the history of Jesus nor any metaphysical account of divine sonship seems to me to be possible for us in any other form. But the story has its roots in what happened—hence the value of the reference to 'suffered under Pontius Pilate' in the creed; and the story points us truly, I believe, in the direction of a valid apprehension and worship of God—hence the value of speaking of Jesus as Son of God. But, as with so many of the credal affirmations, we cannot disentangle the history from the interpretative pictures in terms of which it has come down to us. In this sphere as in others critical study seeks to analyse the complex story. But it does so not in order simply to dissolve and to destroy, but rather that by seeing the component parts more clearly we may ultimately be enabled to grasp the nature of the whole more truly. For it is by living within and in response to that whole that our lives are sustained and built up in the worship and obedience of God.

7

A. M. Allchin

It is the ninth century in what we now call Iraq. A Nestorian bishop is about to die.

And our holy father Mar Abraham the Catholicos told me, saying, 'While many of us were gathered together about him at the hour of his departure, he sat and spake with us concerning his separation from us. And he commanded us to say the response of Baptism. "The doors of the spiritual marriage chamber are opened for the absolution of men", while he sat with his hands laid upon his knees. And when we had come to the passage, "Enter in then ye that are called to the joy which has been prepared for you", he opened his mouth three times to join in the singing, and his soul departed from his body with the joy that was prepared for him. And marvelling, we understood that he actually saw and beheld with the hidden eye of his mind the happiness which had been prepared for him, and that it was because of this he had asked us to sing the baptismal response.'

The words of the hymn which they were singing were as follows,

Open unto me the gates of righteousness—the gates of heaven are opened. The gates of the spiritual marriage chamber of the Bridegroom are opened for the forgiveness of the sins of men, and through the gift of the Spirit from on high, mercy and peace are now vouchsafed to all mankind. Enter in therefore, O ye who are called; enter into the joy which is prepared for you, and with pure and sanctified heart and true faith, give thanks to Christ our Saviour . . . O thou true Door open to the lost and call us to enter the treasury on high.[1]

Now the scene is England in the seventeenth century. At Little Gidding the family are gathering around the death bed of Nicholas Ferrar.

1 *The Book of Governors. The Historia Monastica of Thomas, Bishop of Marga* (A.D. 840), ed. E. A. Wallis Budge, vol. II, pp. 518–19.

Towards evening he called the family and other friends together . . . and asked them to say the prayers for a dying man. He seemed to fall into a peaceful sleep for a time, but they remained with him in the room. Suddenly he raised himself up in bed. His voice came clear and strong and, stretching out his arms, he looked upwards and around him with a light of great happiness in his eyes.

'O what a blessed change is here,' he cried. 'What do I see. . . . I have been at a great feast. O, magnify the Lord with me!'

One of his nieces spoke to him.

'At a feast, dear Father?'

'Ay,' he answered, 'at a great feast, the great King's feast.'

They stood in awe waiting for him to continue. But he sank back quietly on his bed and closed his eyes. . . . His lips parted and he gave a long gasp. In that moment they saw that his soul was sped. At the same instant the clock struck one; it was the hour at which for years past he had always risen for his morning devotions.[1]

Here are two incidents from widely separated times and places. They speak to us of, what David Jones calls, the 'inward continuities', which run through all the evident discontinuities of man's history. They help us to remember and recollect the scattered fragments of our being, and to make a liberating and life-giving *anamnesis*.[2] They unite us with the gospel itself, which at its heart contains the proclamation of a great joy, the news of a Kingdom and a Feast, present and yet to come, the mystery of a passage from death into life, in which sin and death are overcome, and all that binds down and destroys man's life is finally defeated. The life which is there made free, though rooted in space and time, evidently has its issues in a world which goes beyond this universe in which we customarily live and move and have our being. Man's origin and final destiny is greater than that.

It is one of the agreed features of the discussion which has taken place in the formulation of this report, that there must be a dialogue, an interchange between what is given in the Bible and tradition, and the findings and the questionings of the present day. Much of the

1 A. L. Maycock, *Nicholas Ferrar of Little Gidding*, pp. 299–300.
2 Many scholars think that the Greek word *anamnesis* in Scripture has a more active meaning than the words 'remembrance' or 'memorial', which would translate it, normally have. It suggests not just the recalling of something now absent, but the bringing into the present of a past reality, so that it becomes 'here and now operative in its effects' (cf., e.g., Gregory Dix, *The Shape of the Liturgy*, p. 161).

disagreement which has emerged in our discussion has turned on the question of the balance and emphasis of that dialogue. Are we adapting ourselves and our own presuppositions to the givenness of the tradition, or are we adapting the tradition to the needs and requirements of ourselves and our contemporaries? How is the give and take to go? Are we finally to accommodate the mysteries of God's revelation to our own fallen capacities, or are we to look for some transformation of man's heart and mind, so that we, in all the finitude of our being, may be made apt to perceive something of the infinite glory of the Divine?

Another way of posing this question is to ask whether the Church, in its fullness, is something which needs to be fitted into this world or whether the world is something which needs to be caught up into the kingdom through the Church?

The term *Katholike* or *Catholica* in the Fathers of the early centuries, when used as a noun, is often synonymous with *Ecclesia* to designate a new reality which is not a part of the cosmos, but a totality of a more absolute order. It exists in the world, but the world cannot contain it. 'The place is too narrow for me; make room for me to dwell in'; for St Gregory of Nyssa these words of the prophecy of Isaiah (49.20) are the words of the Church. For St Ambrose, the Church is greater than the earth and the sky. It is a new world which has Christ for its sun. It contains the whole inhabited earth, for all are called to become one in Christ, and even now it is the Church which is this new totality.[1]

But it is not only the Church which says, 'The place is too narrow for me.' Every human being is called to say the same, in so far as he is being released from the deformations of individualism, which subject him to death and sin and make space and time into barriers and means of separation, rather than forms of communion in love and knowledge.

In the reality of the fallen world, human beings tend to exist in mutual exclusion, each one affirming himself in opposition to the others, that is to say in dividing up and parcelling out the unity of nature, each one possessing for himself a part of that nature so that *my* will opposes myself to all that is not me. Looked at in this way, what we customarily call a human person is not really a person but an individual, that is to say a part of the common nature, more or less

1 Vladimir Lossky, *In the Image and Likeness of God*, pp. 183–4. Page references are to the English translation of this book, but the passages quoted have been directly translated from the French original.

similar to other parts or human individuals which go to make up humanity. But in so far as he is person in the true sense, in the theological sense of this word, a human being is not limited by his individual nature; he is not only a part of the whole, but each one virtually contains the whole, the totality of the terrestrial world, of which he is the hypostasis; thus each one is the unique, and absolutely original aspect or face of the nature which is common to all. . . . In our habitual experience, we know neither the true diversity of persons, nor the true unity of nature; we see human individuals on the one side, and human collectivities on the other, in perpetual conflict.[1]

The implications of this distinction between person and individual, which is vital if we are to make any sense of the Christian tradition of prayer, are worked out in much greater human detail in many contemporary writers. Thomas Merton, for instance, has very much to say on it, Alan Ecclestone in *Yes to God* has an admirable chapter considering its social and political consequences.

But to see the existence of the Church and the existence of each member of it in this way implies that there must be a very great transformation of our fallen ways of thinking and feeling, of seeing and doing things. Our human nature must be reformed and renewed after the pattern of the divine nature. Personal knowledge always and necessarily involves communion, a sharing of life. If this is true in our relations as between human beings, how much more so is it true in our relationship with God.

To know God one must draw near to him. No one who does not follow the path of union with God can be a theologian. The way of the knowledge of God is necessarily the way of deification. . . . Such an attitude utterly excludes all abstract and purely intellectual theology which would adapt the mysteries of the wisdom of God to human ways of thought. It is an existential attitude which involves the whole man.[2]

Thus theology will never be abstract, working through concepts, but contemplative: raising the mind to those realities which pass all understanding. This is why the dogmas of the Church often present themselves to human reason as antinomies, the more difficult to resolve the more sublime the mystery which they express. It is not a

1 ibid., pp. 106–7.
2 Vladimir Lossky, *The Mystical Theology of the Eastern Church*, pp. 38–9.

question of suppressing the antinomy by adapting dogma to our understanding, but of a change of heart and mind enabling us to attain to the contemplation of the reality which reveals itself to us as it raises us to God, and unites us, according to our several capacities, to him.[1]

Such a view of theology does not dispense its practitioner from all the intellectual rigour of which he is capable. Vladimir Lossky's own work, particularly his extremely close and detailed study of the writings of Meister Eckhart, is proof enough of that. It is only by the utmost use of reason that reason can be transcended. But it will evidently relate the work of the theologian very closely to the work of the man of prayer, and to the work of the one who seeks to find and to serve Christ in all the most unexpected corners of the human and natural creation. It is not by chance that such a vision of the nature of theology should be found in the seventeenth century in Lancelot Andrewes, and again in the nineteenth in Father R. M. Benson. In our own day the scholar and the thinker who follows this path will see his own particular intellectual work as a service of the whole Christian people, an attempt to articulate and make explicit what indeed may be known more deeply though perhaps less vocally by many others than himself. He will be attentive to the saints of his own time, to a Staretz Silvan or a Mother Theresa, no less than to those of the past, as figures who are likely to provide him with much of the basic data, the raw material of his subsequent reflection.

Such a view-point will also make the one who holds it more than a little sceptical of the presuppositions and unquestioned assumptions of the age in which he lives. Far from supposing that we live in an age in some way privileged over other centuries in all fields of knowledge, he will come to suspect that our great and unquestioned advances in certain areas of human knowledge, i.e. the natural sciences, have been purchased at a heavy price, a virtual blindness in other areas of human wisdom, so that things which our forefathers saw so clearly that they hardly needed to speak of them, are now almost wholly closed to us. Let us give two examples from what would generally be regarded as somewhat peripheral areas of Christian doctrine, which because they are not mentioned in the creeds have not been discussed in our report.

1.   *The being and nature of angels*
Certainly no Anglican will be inclined to maintain that it is necessary to

1 ibid., p. 43.

salvation that a man should believe in the existence of angels. Doubtless many would think of it as one of those items of Christian tradition which was eminently expendable. Yet the fact that there are angelic spirits is everywhere presupposed in Scripture, and is an inherent element in the whole Christian tradition of prayer and worship. When we come into the presence of God, we bring with us the praise of the whole of that creation of which we are a part; but we also find ourselves in company with another order of creation, not part of this world of space and time, in which we are at home, yet somehow intervening in it. If we take seriously the belief that the words of the liturgy are no less expressive of the Church's faith than the words of the creed, then we shall at least be led to investigate this question more closely. We may come to reflect that the most commonly used form of Christian prayer, the prayer which is on the lips of Christian people every day all over the world, itself presupposes this belief; for as Richard Hooker remarks,

> as in number and order they are huge, mighty and royal armies, so likewise in perfection of obedience unto that law, which the Highest, whom they adore, love and imitate, hath imposed upon them, such observants they are thereof, that our Saviour himself being to set down the perfect idea of that which we are to pray and wish for on earth, did not teach to pray or wish for more than only that here it might be with us, as with them it is in heaven.

Hooker continues,

> Desire to resemble God in goodness maketh them unweariable and even unsatiable in their longing to do by all means all manner of good unto all the creatures of God, but especially unto the children of men: in the countenance of whose nature, looking downward, they behold themselves beneath themselves; even as upward, in God, beneath whom themselves are, they see that character which is nowhere but in themselves and us resembled. Thus far even the pagans have approached; thus far they have seen into the doings of the angels of God. . . .[1]

That belief in the existence and ministry of angels presents particular difficulties for our age, there is no reason to deny. An order of beings, created like ourselves, but not fitting neatly into the universe which our senses discover to us, is for us a considerable problem. But the universal

---

1 *The Works of Richard Hooker*, ed. John Keble, vol. I. pp. 212–13. (*The Laws of Eccles. Pol.*, Book I. iv. i.)

conviction not only of the Christian tradition, but also, as Hooker remarks, of all the religious traditions of mankind, may well give us pause. Certainly here we shall question, be as sceptical as we may be, we shall seek to reinterpret and to reunderstand, in the light of our modern discoveries about the universe and about the nature of man. But we shall do it from within the tradition, not from without. We shall not be inclined lightly either to abandon or reject an element of the faith, which far from being a burden may prove to be a source of insight and of joy. We may even remember that Richard Hooker himself, a man as F. D. Maurice remarks, 'who knew a thousand times as much of Church controversies as any of us know—and was a better logician as well as a more devout man than I suppose any of us would pretend to be . . .', chose to meditate on this very subject of the service and hierarchy of the angels as he came to the end of his brief but so fruitful life.

2.   The perpetual virginity of Mary

If, as is clear for many Anglicans, belief in the existence and ministry of angels seems superfluous and expendable, then it is equally evident that belief that Mary the Mother of God was virgin not only before the birth of her son, but also remained so afterwards, will seem even more unnecessary and indefensible. Indeed, as is clear both from the work of this Doctrine Commission, and of the Commission which met between the two wars, belief in the Virgin Birth itself is more and more questioned in our Church. To the theological attitude represented in this essay, the argument that the New Testament evidence for the Virgin Birth is insufficient, though a comprehensible one, appears singularly unconvincing. The evidence of St Matthew and St Luke, when taken in conjunction with the consensus of the whole tradition at least until the nineteenth century, seems overwhelmingly strong. At any rate it is not this point which we are arguing here. We are concerned with the question of whether after the birth of her firstborn son Mary should have gone on to have had other children. The evidence of the Gospels, in speaking about the brothers and sisters of Jesus, would at first sight suggest that the answer is Yes. But the term 'ever-virgin' almost as firmly rooted in the tradition as the title 'Mother of God' would suggest the answer No. What are we to make of this contradiction?

In the first place it must be said that the whole area of teaching about Mary, at least in the mind of the early centuries and of the Orthodox Church to this day, constitutes, as it were, a secondary realm of reflection and insight, subsequent upon the primary proclamation of the things concerning Jesus. It is for this reason that the Marian definitions made by the Roman Catholic Church in the last century and a half are to be regretted. They have pushed into public definition things which belong to the Church's inner awareness. So here is a matter where the believer may prefer a certain silent agnosticism, not denying nor too readily affirming, but waiting (like William Temple in the case of the Virgin Birth itself) for the growth of insight and understanding. Meanwhile, we may remark that the suggestion of many of the Fathers that the brethren of Jesus referred to in the Gospels were children of Joseph by a previous marriage, is not so implausible as it is sometimes said to be. Had Jesus had younger brothers, it is at least curious that he should have had so little influence upon them during the years of his ministry. But further than this, it will seem that the conviction that Mary remained ever virgin is one which grew and ripened through centuries of reflection upon the way in which God acts in and through man. The term is not the result of an antagonism to human sexuality, though we know that that has at times invaded the Church, but of a deep insight into the way in which God works in human life, an insight given to those who have known in flesh and blood more of what this means than we or most of our contemporaries do. Is it to be thought that she who is 'greater than the heavens', since she contained the Creator of the heavens, is in her own life wholly subject to the law of sin and death which is broken by her Son? Here again a respect for the tradition may open to us a fullness of love and understanding, where too hasty a decision would shut us up within the framework of our own limited and distorted world-view. The question when rightly posed is not what do we have, however grudgingly, to believe in order to arrive at an essential minimum, but how is it that we can enter into that fullness of faith and insight which alone will allow man's life to grow to its true stature of love and knowledge in the power and grace of God?

For we must move from the periphery of Christian doctrine, though in the coinherence of all teachings with one another it is perhaps inaccurate to speak of any detail of the tradition as peripheral, to the very centre, to the point of Christ's conquest over death by death. That the event of Christ's rising from the dead will not fit into our ordinary historical categories is not surprising. In fact it could not have been new life from the tomb if it had done. By its very nature this central mystery must break open the categories of human thinking, just as it breaks down the barriers of sin and death, and reconciles all men with one another in reconciling them with God. It could not do this unless it had indeed actually happened at a certain place and in a certain time, unless indeed the grave were empty and Christ were risen in the fullness of his humanity. But no event is less imprisoned within the particular moment in which it takes place. It stretches back no less than forwards in time to include all humanity and all creation in its embrace.

A clue to its interpretation is given in the Orthodox icon of the resurrection, which depicts what in the West has commonly been called the harrowing of hell; Christ descending among the dead draws up Adam and Eve, the representatives of all humanity, out of darkness into light. By comparison the medieval Western paintings of a solitary Christ stepping out of the grave, whatever their artistic beauty, seem theologically disastrous. They break the solidarity of Christ with all mankind, and suggest an understanding of the resurrection which sees it as an afterthought, rather than the very substance of Christ's conflict with the powers of death. In an age like our own which is haunted by images of meaninglessness and corruption, by fears that God is absent or dead, the mystery of the descent into hell, the conquest of death by death takes on all its power and meaning. The verses in St Matthew's Gospel (27.50–3) which speak of the rending of the veil of the temple, the earthquake and the opening of the graves at the moment of Jesus' death, though they are doubtless hard of interpretation, are surely vitally significant. They speak of the cosmic dimensions of this moment when Christ dies, and affirm the immediate and universal consequences of this death.

In the one man, in whom all mankind is renewed, because all mankind is united with God, the powers of death are overcome, the Kingdom of Heaven is opened to all who believe; 'and through the gift of the Spirit from on high, mercy and peace are now vouchsafed to all mankind'. For on the mystery of death and resurrection there follows the mystery of the coming of the Spirit at Pentecost. It is in the coming of the Spirit that the once-for-all events of Christ are communicated to men of every age and every place, and that the Church is established in the unshakeable certainty of the communion which the Spirit brings. It is this activity of the Holy Spirit which makes possible the communication of the gospel, and breaks down the barriers which separate us from the past of the Church and from the brief years of Jesus' earthly ministry. 'He will teach you all things, and bring to your remembrance all that I have said to you' (John 14.26).

This 'he will bring all things to your remembrance' is addressed not only to the apostles who accompanied Jesus Christ from the very beginning, but also to all Christians, all the members of the Church who have a common memory of the words of Christ, of what was 'from the beginning': a memory which is called Tradition. This memory is common to all; it belongs to the unity of the Body of Christ, the Church; it is its memory or tradition but it is actualised in each particular person upon whom the Holy Spirit confers his grace.[1]

It is the particular witness of the Anglican churches in the years since the Reformation that they constantly look beyond themselves to that greater whole of which they are a part, to the unity of the Body of Christ. In the words of Herbert Thorndike in the seventeenth century, we appeal to 'the Scriptures interpreted by the perpetual practice of God's Church', or of R. M. Benson in the nineteenth century, 'There is no particular reason why we should be loyal to any particular age. Our loyalty is due to truth and to the great principle of truth which the Church of England enunciated, the tradition of the undivided Church.' That there is difficulty in maintaining this position for a Church which itself is conscious of being, at some levels, divided from the centres of the tradition, the form and content of this report make clear. Yet even the uncertainties and tensions, the pains and travail may have a positive meaning. In the words of Michael Ramsey in our own century, the vindication of the Anglican tradition lies

in its pointing through its own history to something of which it is a fragment. Its credentials are its incompleteness, with the tension and travail in its soul. It is clumsy and untidy, it baffles neatness and logic. For it is sent not to commend itself as 'the best type of Christianity', but by its very brokenness to point to the universal Church wherein all have died.[2]

It is only as we abide in the unity of faith and hope and love, with all those who through the gift of the Spirit share a common memory of the words and deeds of Christ, a common knowledge of his death in which all have died, his rising in which all are made alive, that we shall be able to know the truth, the truth which makes man free.

Let us again insist that the question before us is not one of finding some irreducible minimum without which a man could no longer call himself a Christian, but of entering into that fullness of life and truth

1 *In the Image and Likeness of God*, pp. 191–2.
2 A. M. Ramsey, *The Gospel and the Catholic Church*, p. 220.

without which we shall never begin to live with the freedom of the children of God. The work of the theologian is not one of reduction, but of discrimination. There is an order or hierarchy within the body of Christian doctrines, and although all the elements of the faith are precious and nothing to be refused, there are certainly distinctions to be made between things essential and things less essential, between dogmas publicly proclaimed and articles to be reflected upon in silence. Much of the particular work of our own tradition in the years since the sixteenth century has been to make these discriminations and to try to recognize these gradations. But this work itself must be carried on within the tradition of prayer and faith articulated and developed in the years before the great schism of East and West. It must never delude us into thinking that the truth of God is something which we hold and over which we have power, instead of remembering always that it is a truth which maintains and upholds us. Our work is one of discernment not accommodation. 'Adapt yourselves no longer to the pattern of this present world, but let your minds be remade and your whole nature thus transformed. Then you will be able to discern the will of God, and to know what is good, acceptable, and perfect' (Rom. 12.2).

In a retreat given to the community at Cowley in 1876, R. M. Benson put it like this.

> The relationship between ourselves and truth is something very much more than a mere intellectual question of truth . . . We fancy that we are approaching the truth because we speak formularies of truth, but those formularies of truth are not the truth. They are mere expressions in which the truth is formulated for our acceptance; whereas the truth is the very law and power of our lives. . . . Christian dogma is often spoken of as very dead and dry; and indeed as men are apt to fight for it, it is dead and dry, and being dead and dry it has lost its very Christianity. It remains a dogma, but no more like the original dogma of the faith than is the husk that lies upon the ground identical with the fruit once found upon the tree . . . We must know the truth as a mighty power having its own organisation . . . giving itself not so much to us, but rather taking us into itself. . . . Thus we can see how 'the Church is the pillar and ground of the truth', not merely because the Church retains and authenticates certain books as of canonical authority, not merely because the Church is capable of speaking age after age with a determinate utterance when men's minds are in doubt. . . . The Church is the

pillar and ground of truth not merely because she exists in the world as a Divine oracle, but because her life is the life of God, because she is instinct with the powers of God, because her mind is identified with the mind of God, because she breathes with the breath of the eternal Spirit of God, because her hopes rise up beyond the measure of this lower world, and find no satisfaction save in the perfect glory of God. . . . She is no mere record of a life to be found elsewhere, but she is the embodiment of that to which she testifies. And so 'we must know the truth and the truth shall make us free', while we really live as the children of this incarnation; while we really live in the power of this Divine Breath, while we really live in the glory of this holy Church, the pillar and ground of the truth, the Body of Christ.[1]

'The place is too narrow for me; make room for me to dwell in.' . . . 'The gates of the spiritual marriage chamber of the Bridegroom are opened for the forgiveness of the sins of man.' The Kingdom is very near, present amongst us; already the powers of the age to come press into the confines of time and space. And in our own century, as the whole human race enters into a new closeness of contact at every level of human life, something more of the full dimension of that Kingdom opened to us by Christ's conquest over death by death begins to become evident. In the rapid and radical transformations of man's life and consciousness at present going on, in the search which is everywhere taking place for the true liberation of man and the rediscovery of human unity, this world appears to approach a moment of crisis. At such a moment the whole Church needs to be able to enter into and live by the fullness of the tradition of life and wisdom which it has received, so that it may respond with genuine creativity to the demands and opportunities which this time presents to us.

1 From the MS Volume of Retreat Addresses (1876), pp. 32–3. A fuller quotation is to be found in A. M. Allchin, *The Spirit and the World*, pp. 41–6.

8

Hugh Montefiore

There is a great variety of ways in which people become Christians. Some like myself are introduced to Christianity through a sudden and intimately personal experience irrupting into consciousness; and it is only later that reflection takes place, and intellectual problems of theology arise. The case may not be so very different for some who have been brought up within the Christian Church. From infancy and childhood they may have been nurtured within the community of faith in such a way that they have thought little about their beliefs until adulthood, when (especially if they are intellectuals) they may begin to examine the doctrinal contents of their faith.

It is only natural that this should happen, for curiosity is a characteristic of the higher mammals, and one of the distinguishing characteristics of *homo sapiens* is a propensity for intellectual curiosity. All intelligent Christians should feel the claim upon them of rigorous intellectual honesty, and when this is combined with a sharpened intellectual curiosity, the result is a passionate search for truth. Christian theology is the product of such a passion.

There are, however, different kinds of truth, and theological truth differs from other kinds. A true statement is usually understood to be one which corresponds to what is the case, or that which is internally self-consistent, and coherent with other truths. But a theological statement cannot precisely tell me what is the case, for the subject of theology is God, and my finite contingent intellect cannot precisely comprehend what is infinite and necessary: I cannot, for example, know just what I mean if I assert that God is love. Even analogical statements about God lack precision (implying, for example, that God's love is to God as human love is to a human being), because by their very nature the precise relationship between God and human beings in such a statement remains mysterious. I can try to describe my relationship to God but I cannot precisely define it.

What then am I doing when I make a statement about God? Theological statements are models, or more usually they contain a combination of differing models in a sophisticated interrelationship, through which different aspects of the reality of God may be conceptualized and thus communicated. I cannot hope that any theological statement that I make about God can be fully adequate to his reality, nor can I necessarily expect a completely logical self-consistency or coherence in a theological statement, or in a series of such statements. For if I am trying to conceptualize a Reality who lies beyond the signification of human language and for whom no adequate human models of thought can exist, then I may have to be content with seeming paradox and inconsistency. Even in the subatomic sciences (in the cases of light and matter, for example) description through analogies and symbols may give rise to apparently paradoxical statements; and *a fortiori* in theological statements, where different aspects of divine activity may require different and to some extent contradictory models, some degree of paradox is to be expected.

How then am I to find some criterion by which I can theologize? How am I to decide what is true from what is false? Can a distinction be made between orthodoxy and heresy, or is the distinction no longer valid?

The ultimate criterion of any theological statement is for me its *adequacy*. It must be adequate to satisfy all the evidence that I can accept, and my interpretation of that evidence. What evidence can I accept? To begin with, a theological statement of belief must be adequate to my experience (such as it has been) and to my interpretation of that experience. For example, I could not accept that the religious experience that inaugurated my Christian commitment was delusory. Although I may interpret it as clothed in the imagery appropriate to my condition at the time, any interpretation which denies its transcendental origin is for me inadequate. Similarly, any expression of my belief must be adequate to the grace which I have received as a Christian through word and sacrament.

Again, such an expression of faith must be adequate to my understanding of the world of nature and of people; that is to say, it must be congruous with the truth as I understand this through the natural sciences, and as I encounter it in the world in which I live. For example, since human personality is formed through the pairing of twenty-three male and twenty-three female chromosomes, I find that I can best assert the orthodox dogma of Jesus' full humanity by interpreting the credal phrases 'conceived by the Holy Ghost, born of the Virgin Mary' in what are for me very real and meaningful but non-literal and symbolic senses; and similarly I interpret the phrase 'from whence he shall come to judge the quick and the dead' in an equally real but non-literal and symbolic sense in the light of the scientific hypothesis that in some 10^{10} years the sun will become a red giant and swallow up the earth.

Again, a theological statement of my belief must be adequate to what is known through the behavioural sciences about social and psychological factors affecting belief. Although these cannot prove or disprove the truth or validity of my religious faith, they can force me into a rigorous self-examination, challenging me to ask whether my judgement about what is true has been affected by my psychological neeed to assert it as true. These social and psychological factors themselves produce a criterion of adequacy: 'What kind of God has created a world in which laws of this kind operate about our beliefs concerning him?'

One important question to be asked about religious beliefs focused on an historical person is this: 'Is there an adequate historical base on which these beliefs about an historical person can rest?' Although this vast subject must be pursued in detail with the greatest possible rigour of historical and literary inquiry, the actual questions that I need to ask myself may be reduced to two only: 'Is there adequate evidence to establish the personal character which Jesus must have had to give rise to these Gospels about him?' and 'Is the evidence of the Gospels adequate as a base on which to ground the Christian belief in his crucifixion and resurrection?' I do not have to convince myself that *proof* can be found from these sources, but simply that other explanations of the Gospel evidence are more inadequate than affirmatory replies to these questions.

Another aspect of the criterion of adequacy assumes particular importance for me because of my Jewish background. I was nurtured with a lively faith in the same one God in whom I still believe, and I cannot deny my origins. In any case I find much evidence of a genuine relationship of faith on the part of members of religions other than the one which I profess; and when (as I wish to do) I assert the uniqueness and exclusiveness of Jesus Christ, what I say must be adequate to the reality of religious experience on the part of those who are not his adherents.

At first sight it might seem that these criteria of adequacy leave me with only a subjective version of the Christian faith. This subjective aspect is inherent in any form of personal belief. A man can only believe what he does believe, and he cannot force himself to accept something that he believes to be untrue, and even if he accepts a belief on the authority of an institution or of another person, there is a subjective aspect to his belief in their authority. But a man's faith is not simply his own. I have received mine through others, and it has been nurtured within the fellowship of the Church. It is intrinsically improbable that the truth about the Christian faith (or of a particular doctrine of the Christian faith) has been hidden down the centuries but has been only lately revealed to me. I share my faith with others, and to disown their fundamental convictions is to cut myself off from the community of faith to which I belong. No doubt the whole question of faith looks very different to someone who lives outside this fellowship of faith; but the existence of unbelievers and agnostics—a factor I must take into account when testing my faith—does not alter for me the adequacy of faith as a response to life.

A crucial test of adequacy is the relationship of my own beliefs to those of mainstream Christianity down the centuries, especially to the theological expressions of belief to be found in holy Scripture. The very possibility of an appeal beyond Scripture rules out the Bible as my only or even my highest guide, for if there is even one occasion when I do not accept its overriding authority, then there must be some criterion higher than Scripture to which I can appeal. On the other hand, the evidence forces me to give a very high authority indeed to the contents of the New Testament, not only as a result of critical study, but also because its words so often speak to my whole self—at the deep levels of will and feelings and imagination as well as at the ratiocinative and discursive levels of mind. When read or heard in a discriminating way, passages from the Bible (including the Old as well as the New Testament) can not only illumine my path but also become for me, as for others, a vehicle of the Holy Spirit. Yet the Bible does not claim inerrancy for itself and I have no reason to suppose it is inerrant. Moreover, I would expect that within a broad spectrum of theological agreement there exists some theological pluralism; and that is what I find even in the New Testament. I cannot suppose that its contents will be free from cultural relativism, so that I may expect to 'translate' or 'remythologize' its thought forms and imagery in order to reformulate for myself the truths which the sacred writers were trying to express when they wrote as they did.

Scripture is the source of Christian tradition, which flows down the centuries to the present, beginning from the original witnesses of the events which were constitutive of the Church. Within this mainstream there have been many different currents and bifurcations, and there are few doctrinal formulations that can claim recognition by a rigorous application of the Vincentian canon *quod semper, quod ubique, quod ab omnibus* (always, everywhere, and by all). None the less, the chief theological affirmations which the Church has held in common far outweigh in importance the differences which are the product of a theological pluralism such as has always existed within Christendom, even when there appeared outwardly to be conformity. Although I may have to reinterpret them afresh for today, I dare not deny these main theological affirmations which the Church has always held without cutting myself off from mainstream Christianity. Yet I cannot expect my own formulated beliefs to be the same as those held in past ages, because I accept the fact of a certain cultural relativism; I think differently from others because I live within a particular context of culture. Nor can I expect to hold the same beliefs as all other Christians, not because I believe that truth is unimportant, but because I realize that the apprehension of truth by each person is determined to a certain extent by his psychological temperament, and also by the environment in which he has been nurtured and in which he now lives.

I must ask myself: is there in fact any substantial subject of faith at all? My basic affirmation is that of Being beyond all being and within all being. It is an affirmation that the world has meaning and value in itself, and is not a mere random concatenation of atoms and energy, unexplained and inexplicable. It is an act of faith in reality at its deepest level and in the rationality and righteousness of the universe. This fundamental affirmation exemplifies the manysidedness of the criterion of adequacy. It is not for me a matter of mere argumentation—the Five Ways of St Thomas Aquinas cannot prove the existence of God—nor can such a conclusion be read off from the natural or behavioural sciences: signals of transcendence, for example, can be at best 'rumours of angels', not proofs of God. It is a convergence of evidence that justifies my religious affirmation about God: any other attempt to interpret life is not less but more inadequate to explain all the evidence, including the phenomena of man's religious experience and the deepest needs of his psyche for challenge and security. But I do not in fact believe in God because it is reasonable to do so, or even because I find it the least inadequate interpretation of existence, however convincing this way of thinking may appear. I believe because I am caught up in a community of faith which has many aspects. It is when I am assailed by doubt whether I ought to go on believing that I ask myself what is more adequate to the situation, to believe, to disbelieve, or to suspend belief? I must take into account my own religious experience, that of my fellow-Christians from New Testament times down the ages, as well as the theistic beliefs and testimony of adherents to other faiths. I must ask myself whether this experience of God which I share with others is best regarded as illusory or indicative of divine Reality. I evaluate as best I may the evidences of religious psychology, I look at the form and content of contingent existence, the mysteries of energy and matter in subatomic structures and in inter-galactic space. I ask myself about the adequacy of a reductionist interpretation of truth, beauty, goodness, and love. I find that the affirmation of God is a more adequate response to all this than any other.

Out of this basic affirmation about God springs the whole of my doctrinal structure of belief. If I affirm God, I must affirm him as personal, or at least as not less than personal, because he cannot be less than his own creation. Inasmuch as he is the creator and sustainer of everything, I would expect to find within his universe the creativity and regularity which the evolutionary process in fact provides. Because there is personality in God and he is transcendent over his universe, I apply to him the human model of fatherhood. Because he is God, he is one; for two Gods form a contradiction in terms. But unity is not necessarily a simple concept. When I contemplate the complexity and dynamism of our evolving universe, together with the suffering experienced by the sentient life within it, a bare static monism which affirms the Unmoved Mover is for me inadequate as its explanation. A trinitarian faith (whatever be the metaphysical mystery which underlies it) is less inadequate to my experience of God and of his world.

God is almighty in the sense that as Creator and Sustainer he is responsible for everything that is and for all beings who have emerged. He is therefore responsible for the evil in the world; and I would expect him to take special steps on behalf of those beset by it as I find that he has done through Jesus of Nazareth. Because love is the highest experience of human life, and stands at the apex of human values, I must suppose that God's nature is best likened to the model of human love, and that he would use love to overcome evil; and this is what is disclosed to me through Jesus. In fact the very notion of God is so obscure, and so beyond my human comprehension, that it seems congruous with his nature, if he is love, to disclose himself to me through a medium which I can understand; and this too is what is disclosed to me through Jesus. If God used matter and energy as the vehicle of himself, then it seems to follow that these are fundamentally good in themselves, and that God's mode of operation within his universe is likely to be sacramental, i.e. using the physical and material as the medium and means of his spiritual action within his world. If God's nature is love, it would also seem congruous not only that he should disclose himself to all people who are capable of response to him, but that he should also make a personal self-disclosure through the only medium which human beings really understand—that is, through human personality. If God's nature is love, it would also seem congruous that he should wish to share this love with created beings, that in his providence beings capable of participating in his nature should emerge, and that he should enable them to respond. All this I believe to have been disclosed to be the case.

This, in brief, is my formal outline of faith. Christology does not alter my doctrine of God; it clarifies and defines it. The teaching of Christ is not true because Christ taught it: he taught it because it is true. Christ did not reveal a new face of God. He came to disclose the eternal face of God so far as human personality is capable of disclosing it, and by his life, death, and resurrection to effect that reconciliation between God and man which the Divine Will always strives to effect. God wills to be incarnate in all his creatures, and to effect universal reconciliation within his creation: in Jesus his will was fully and uniquely realized.

This historical account of Jesus, in so far as it can be recovered from the Gospels, is subject to strict historical inquiry, and so are the previous events of Jewish history which culminated in his ministry. Although we have not histories of Jesus, but Gospels which interpret his ministry and are coloured by the later experience of the Church, yet in my judgement the character of Jesus shines clear through the records, and the main events of his ministry and the outline of his teaching can be discerned. I cannot explain away the 'miraculous' aspects of the Gospels as fictitious on *a priori* grounds, for the proven existence of paranormal phenomena suggests a more open approach. The idea that the early Church (for the best of reasons, perhaps, and to a large extent unconsciously) may have fabricated the evidence of the Gospels is to me a far less adequate hypothesis than that the historical person of Jesus, with the character depicted in the Gospels, was the creative force which gave rise to the records. His character is to me self-authenticating, as it has been for millions of others. Mere historical reconstruction by itself can only inform us about earlier events and people. It is the coincidence of history and divinely inspired interpretation of it that gives a disclosure of God working within it. So far as the person of Jesus is concerned, this divinely inspired interpretation, shared within the fellowship of the Church, is the combination of three factors: his own self-understanding, expressed in the Gospels and elaborated in the rest of the New Testament; the impact of his character on my consciousness, whereby I acknowledge him as a man uniquely and divinely inspired to disclose God and to make God present; and my personal experience through which I find that he still influences my life today. And so for me he is not only Jesus of Nazareth, but also the risen Lord.

How am I to interpret this mystery to myself and to others? Various models suggest themselves as the least inadequate and provisional modes of explanation. I think of God's energy active throughout his universe, and uniquely active in the life, death, and resurrection of Jesus. The mystery of Christ's divinity can perhaps best be understood by thinking of the moving pattern of divine activity coincident with and focused in the human life of Jesus, and by interpreting the union of human and divine in Jesus after the model of human free will and divine grace. Jesus' death on the cross can perhaps best be understood as God's acceptance of the worst evil of the world which he has created. In the god-forsakenness of Jesus on the cross and in the accursed nature of his death, God was at work so as to open up life and freedom to those whose lives become a desolation and a hell. Through his acceptance of the worst that men can do, God gives an assurance that all men, however bad, are accepted by his love. By his conquest of death on Easter Sunday, God affirmed the ultimate victory of love and truth over evil and falsehood, and embraced all men within this act of redemption.

There remain, of course, many problems and mysteries. For example, in what respects did the particular human nature of Jesus act as the medium of divine self-disclosure? We can only speculate; and such speculations (although regrettably they can cause great distress when distorted by the mass media of communication) are for me a necessary outcome of a genuine search for religious truth; for without speculation there can be no advance in religious understanding.

Christology is the focal element of Christian belief; but it forms only one part of a total doctrinal structure. Whatever may have been the physical manifestations of Christ's resurrection, they attest the power and propriety of his death. The death and resurrection of Jesus give us one of the deepest insights into the nature of reality. Christ died and rose again because the combination of love and faithfulness to truth, when they appear most powerless, are in fact victorious. The resurrection of Christ is not just a past event, but he is alive and active in the world. His Spirit, which is active throughout the evolving universe, and which gives to human beings their special worth, energizes the Church, which despite its human and therefore sinful aspect, is of divine appointment: it is the means through which the gospel has been made known and the setting in which it is lived. Within the Church grace has been given to needy Christians through word and sacrament. The Bible is not only an essential source book of origins, but also—despite the 'occasional' character of much of its contents and the cultural relativism within its pages—an inspired collection of books through which God can make himself known to men. The gospel sacraments of Baptism and Eucharist inaugurate and continue the Christian's relationship to Christ in a sacramental mode. The apostolic ministry is to represent Christ to the Church and the Church to Christ; and this apostolic ministry, no less than the apostolic scriptures, while not essential to the Church's life, is a gift which the Church cannot afford to be without. None the less, it becomes more dispensable as people become more and more mature. But the immaturity of Christians is a sign that God's purpose is incomplete in this world. The divine intention in creation, redemption, and sanctification embraces the whole world, not just mankind: it includes the fitting of human beings to share eternally in the divine life of love and joy; and for this the process of development continues after death. The Church therefore does not exist for itself, but to serve the true needs of all the world; to help to create a society where men and women can fully develop; and to help individuals within it towards a ripeness of life and character to fit them for everlasting life.

Such, in broad outline, is the particular doctrinal framework to which I myself presently subscribe, and which within the confines of this short paper can only summarily be described. Such a doctrinal position, however, can only be provisional. No interpretation of belief can do justice to the Reality which it seeks to express. Moreover, my understanding of truth can change and (I hope) develop; better models can be employed; a rapidly changing culture can result in changed ways of thinking; errors can be purged and mistakes corrected. What is true for me now was not true for me twenty years ago; and, what is more, it is not true for others now. Without in any way abandoning my own convictions—what is true for me now—I must admit the fact of theological pluralism. All doctrinal systems are therefore only provisional.

Then what security of belief can I have? 'General Councils . . . may err, and sometimes have erred, even in things pertaining to God.' However, dogmas of the Church, which are accepted universally (or nearly universally) within the mainstream churches, will have very great authority. (I suppose it is possible that I might want to repudiate such dogmas as are contained in the Apostles' Creed or the Chalcedonian Definition, but if I did so I would not feel able to continue to hold office within the Church.) And yet there are grave difficulties that prevent an unreserved and *ex animo* acceptance of all the Church's dogmas as the personal expression of my own convictions. In the first place, dogmas are written in the language and thought forms of the age that defined them, and these may be different from my own (e.g. the use and meaning of *homoousios*, 'of one substance'). Secondly, every formulation of faith is 'imperfect, incomplete, partial and fragmentary'. Usually they have a polemical bias: they are responses to questions which may be framed very differently today. What a true statement says is true; but what it fails to say may also be true. Theological statements are propositional in form and dialectical in character. The mystery of God is such that any propositional statement which we make about him needs qualification.

The formulation of a dogma, therefore, does not mean that truth has been defined: it means that, through dogmatic assertion, the boundaries of doctrinal formulation have been delineated in such a way as to guard against heresy (that is, an unbalanced formulation of belief), and to open up the possibilities of new doctrinal interpretation. I therefore approach the Church's dogmas with the greatest respect, and (particularly in my episcopal capacity as the Church's representative, which I can never fully divorce from my private life) I can reinterpret but never repudiate or refute them. That does not mean that I must necessarily assert them *ex animo*. They are a stimulus to my renewed attempts to interpret my belief in a way that is intellectually rigorous, personally satisfying, and pastorally relevant. Dogmas are profoundly important as guidelines to the Church's thinking, and as safeguards against heresy and error.

Yet, even in granting as much as this to doctrine and dogma, I have to enter into the cloud of unknowing, and to assert the Church's apophatic tradition. In the suspension of my critical faculties of mind and in the opening of myself to the living God in an attitude of contemplative prayer I know him more truly than in any intellectual proposition about him. Before the mystery of the Divine Presence and Energy all doctrinal reasoning seems as inadequate as the babblings of an infant to the apprehension of an adult. We know only the outskirts of God's ways, and in the silence of concentrated attention the soul can grasp what the mind can never comprehend. Whenever the mind affirms that it understands some truth about God, the soul must also cry out that in the abyss of silence and nothingness a man can find a more authentic affirmation of his religious faith.

But something must be said. Truth needs to be communicated. Experience needs to be shared. The facts of an historical faith need to be known. Very well; but my present understanding of God is only provisional, my present and past experience of God may be superseded, the facts of an historical faith may conceivably be disproved. Have I any commitment which is ultimate?

I commit myself wholly to the living God, the divine Reality who confronts me in my own being and in the world around me and who is transcendent beyond it as well as energetic within it. This living Reality demands my total allegiance. And so too does Jesus. 'And he called unto him the multitude with his disciples, and he said unto them: "If any man would come after me, let him deny himself and take up his cross and follow me."' The call still echoes down the centuries, and with it the power and grace to respond. Following Jesus does not mean primarily believing orthodox propositions about him (although it may involve this); at least it did not mean that during his lifetime. The Apostles did not have to undertake a course of study: they were ordered 'Follow me'. To recite the creed is not the same as to follow Jesus; and in using the creed at baptism we seem to be making a qualifying examination harder than 'finals'. When a young man came to Jesus and wanted to do something more than keep the commandments, he was not ordered to study theology or to learn doctrine: he was told 'Follow me'. To follow Jesus means to adopt his attitudes towards God, towards my fellow men, and towards myself. It has huge implications for my attitudes and practice of prayer and worship, as well as for my deeply held personal and interior feelings of guilt and acceptance, fear and love, anxiety and meaningfulness, disharmony and peace. It has implications too for my outward behaviour, how I react to people and to situations, and what decisions I take. To give my allegiance to God and to follow Jesus affect also my intellectual attitudes. Believing with Jesus that all truth comes from God, I try like Jesus to pursue it wherever it may lead me, and I strive to reconcile secular and religious knowledge. Believing that it is unlikely that God has grievously misled his Church in the past, I do not lightly reject past orthodoxies; believing that others are wiser than myself, I accept the fact of theological pluralism.

I accept the Church's dogmas about Christology, in that I greatly respect them and would not dream of disowning them. I have tried to work out my own beliefs about Jesus in a doctrinal system; but I must admit that it is only provisional. The mystery of Jesus is greater than any formulation about him. I find him as a Person compelling and inescapable, and when he calls me to follow, I can but try to obey. I number myself among those who 'in the toils, the conflicts, the sufferings which they pass through in his fellowship' can learn 'as an ineffable mystery, who he is'. All our dogmas are partial and our doctrines provisional. It is not by these, but by my prayers and my life that, as a disciple of Christ, I make my ultimate affirmation about God, creator, redeemer, and sanctifier.